CLOSE TO THE FLOOR: FOLK DANCE IN NEWFOUNDLAND

CLOSE TO THE FLOOR:
FOLK DANCE IN NEWFOUNDLAND

COLIN QUIGLEY

MEMORIAL UNIVERSITY OF NEWFOUNDLAND
FOLKLORE AND LANGUAGE PUBLICATIONS

MEMORIAL UNIVERSITY OF NEWFOUNDLAND
St. John's, Newfoundland, Canada
1985

Memorial University of Newfoundland
  Folklore and Language Publications
Monograph Series No. 3
General Editors: Herbert Halpert
                   David Buchan
Managing Editor: Martin Lovelace

Available from:
    The Secretary
    Department of Folklore
    Memorial University of Newfoundland
    St. John's, Newfoundland, A1C 5S7
    CANADA

ISBN No. 0-88901-099-4

TABLE OF CONTENTS

ACKNOWLEDGEMENTS

This study has been completed with the help and encouragement of many people. Among them are those who gave generously of their time to teach me something about their dance, music, and way of life. I would like, especially, to thank the Keough and Tracey families, Gerald Quinton, Larry Barker and Lloyd Oldford, who patiently answered my questions, as well as Mrs. Geraldine Keough, in whose home I stayed while working in Plate Cove East. Rufus Guinchard and Emile Benoit, two fine traditional fiddlers, were both very generous with their time and knowledge, as were many other dancers and musicians too numerous to list. I hope my work can contribute in some way to an increased appreciation of their artistry, its transmission and preservation.

I would like to thank both Memorial University and its Department of Folklore for their financial support of my work, through fellowship and field work funds. Throughout my career as a student at Memorial University, I appreciated the encouragement and interest of the faculty of the Department of Folklore; especially the advice and editorial efforts of my thesis supervisor, Neil V. Rosenberg. Herbert Halpert provided references from his collections, as well as editorial comment on some sections of the thesis from which this book has been taken. Wilfred Wareham was generous with his collected material, introductions to potential informants, and personal insight into traditions I was attempting to understand. I could always depend upon David Buchan's support as Department Head during the initial thesis writing and thank him for encouraging this revision of it. In that undertaking Theresa Richard provided patient support. Final editing was performed by Martin Lovelace. I have left many more people unnamed, among them fellow students and friends, but hope that all will accept my sincere gratitude for their interest and help. Any remaining shortcomings are, of course, solely my responsibility.

INTRODUCTION

This book presents an ethnography of the dance traditions which have come to be identified as Newfoundland dance. The vernacular dance traditions in Newfoundland have rarely been recorded, much less systematically described or analyzed. Although they are clearly related to historical dance forms in Britain and their derivatives elsewhere in North America, dance traditions in Newfoundland are distinctive. They reflect the unique characteristics of environment and culture which distinguish this region. My purpose has been to describe the dance movements, social settings, and attitudes which make up these traditions, to examine the relationships among them and their roles as an expressive system. I have not written a history of these dances, although their history is important for an understanding of how they have been used and adapted in rural Newfoundland. Rather, I wish to document the patterns of dance behavior and analyze the expression of cultural values in dance movement.

Because there are so few published descriptions of dance and related aspects of Newfoundland culture, I have included many transcripts from my interviews, and excerpts from archival sources, as well as my own descriptions of the dances. I hope this information will give the reader a feeling for the diversity of actual behavior as well as support my analysis.[1]

A growing number of journal articles, conference papers and more popular media, such as LP record album notes, are beginning to document local traditions in North America. Conspicuous by their absence, however, are studies which unite detailed dance description with movement and contextual analysis in a more complete view of dance behavior within a delimited community. I hope this study will begin to fill that gap.

---

[1]Judith Lynne Hanna, "Toward a Semantic Analysis of Movement Behavior: Concepts and Problems," *Semiotica*, 25 (1978) 99-100, calls for the inclusion of such information.

1

CHAPTER ONE: The People and The Place

My first contact with the folk dance of Newfoundland came in the Spring of 1978 through the CBC television film, "A Time in Red Cliff," which featured several dance performances by individuals who later formed the Red Cliff Dancers.[1] The fast-paced, insistent rhythm of the music, played on accordion and harmonica, and the tremendously energetic dancing were unforgettable and I immediately resolved to learn as much as I could about both. Before coming to Newfoundland I had been playing the fiddle for several years while performing and teaching traditional Anglo-American dances through the Country Dance and Song Society of America, and so found it natural to play with the traditional musicians around St. John's and elsewhere on the island. I tried to learn what people meant when they called for a tune played "close to the floor," or requested me to "double it up" for a step dance. Dancers showed me the figures for "chain up," "round the house," and other parts of the Square Dance, and taught me the "single" and "double" step. I listened to hundreds of tapes in the Memorial University of Newfoundland Folklore and Language Archive and gradually became familiar with the terminology and forms of the Newfoundland traditions. Two years after my initiation I spent several weeks of the summer visiting with people living in the vicinity of that same Red Cliff, on the Bonavista Peninsula, recording their recollections of local dance traditions, learning their steps and tunes from those who still practiced these arts, and participating in contemporary dance events. What I learned of the dance traditions from the people I met there forms the core of this study.[2]

The Keough family of Plate Cove East is one of two prominent musical families in the community; the ability to play an instrument was almost assumed among its members. One of the younger men commented that he had once tried the fiddle because there was music in the family and he thought he'd be able to play.[3] While the transmission of musical traditions within families is commonplace there seems to be a pattern of "inheritance" among public instrumental performers in particular.[4] Michael (Mick) Keough, formerly the leading fiddler in the area, apparently inherited this role from his uncle, Michael (Big Mick) Keough. Big Mick, now deceased, was the leader of most dances in his time, a musician who also taught dances and could "call off" figures to the cotillion.[5] The younger Mick played in his turn for dances in Plate Cove East and West, Open Hall and Tickle Cove. He was born on 28 September 1890 in Plate Cove East, and his father, Patrick Keough, also a fiddler, was born there as well. The family traces its origin to Patrick's grandfather, Andrew, said to have come from County Carlow, Ireland.[6] During his life Mick traveled extensively, working around Grand Falls in the lumber industry; at Sydney, Nova Scotia in the mines; in St. John's "with the Americans"; as well as fishing at home in Plate Cove. One afternoon in June "Mister Mick" related to me the story of how he learned to play:

When I was about thirteen I had a notion of playing then. And anyhow, me father he had a violin one time, and he got sick and ill and he give it all up and he throwed her out into the old back house and she unglued and that. And me uncles . . . . When they thought about who could learn to play they turned to and they got her. And they glued her together and they got her together. And they turned to and they commenced, you know they fiddled her out. They commenced to play, you know. They used to go into the house and here and that. Anyhow me uncle got another violin, a new violin and laid this one to one side. And said, "Take that," he says, "and see would you do anything with it." Anyhow I took it and turned to. And I thought I was made up. Thought I could play. Yes, and here be gar, I busted what strings was on her and I tore the hair out of the bow. And I used to turn to, get pieces of thread and put on her. And anyhow, I used to turn to with a horse would have a long tail. I'd go and cut the tail, the hair off her tail. And used to get it and tie it onto the end of the bow. And turn to and tie it together. And here'd be the big knot in the center. And by and by, be gar, after a spell I commenced to sound out a jig. Commenced to sound out another one. Me brother . . . he had a notion, anyhow, he turned to and he got a rig out. And here we commenced. We commenced to learn . . . . By and by . . . .I got so where I could go to the dances and

4

play and that . . . . Me uncle says, "Boy," he says, "you can play now, but you can put a better sound," he says, "in your violin than I can." "Yes," I says, "you smothers it," I says, "but I don't."[7]

"Fiddler Mick," as he was called, became well known in the region, as the following story illustrates.

Anyhow, I went to a dance one time, mind it was up Southern Bay. Feller was up there playing a 'cordeen [i.e., accordion] and . . . another feller was, he was always being drunk or up dancing. But anyhow all right, I know the tune he was playing was the "Flowers of Edinburgh."

Another man who really could step dance then got out on the floor.

And by and by he stopped, this man. And he come in on the tune again and he went on again and he got to that place and here he, he stopped again. And he said, "I'm giving the floor to you [the first dancer] . . . I'll give the floor to you sir. I can't dance anymore." And he says, "You're the champion now," says, "at the dancing."

Mick, having seen the defeat of the better dancer because of the poor accordion music, invited the loser to hear him play in the back room of the grocery store.

He [the dancer] commenced to foot it out on the floor, step it out. He said, "If I had that," he said, "in there," he says, "I wouldn't let me give the floor to Gun [the other dancer]," And he said, "I don't," he says, "know who you are, but," he says, "would you," he says, "mind just coming and, dancing," says, "playing that for?" "No," I says. I says, "I see your trouble," I says, "in there. I knows your trouble. Yes," I says.

The dancer returned to the dance and asked the dancing master for the floor once again. Gun agreed to "try it again," saying, "I'll get more claps this time."

And anyhow, this feller took the cordeen, you know, and he [the dancer] says "You can put up your cordeen," he says, "You're not playing for me now." And he [the musician] didn't know I was out there see. And he says, "Wait one second," he says, "I'll have somebody to play for me." So I went in with the violin.

Unknown in the community, Mick found "they were look-
ing at me, asking, 'Do you know who?' and said, 'I don't
know.' "

> "Now," I says, "I'll play you," I says, "the whole bar,"
> I says, "to see if it's fast enough." Anyhow he says, "That's
> just," he says, "what I wants." All right so I started. Com-
> menced, you know. And he was going, you know, com-
> menced footing away . . . . And then they commenced
> clapping and clapping and clapping and clapping and clap-
> ping their hands . . . .

Congratulations continued from others in the hall and drinks
of smuggled rum were provided by the winning step dancer.
And according to Mick, "They counted me the best fiddler
on this shore."[8]

Mick's son, Cyril, then forty-seven years old, also played
the violin and knew many of his father's tunes. Cyril never
married and lived with his sister, Therese, their father and
her family. For the last twenty-four years, Cyril worked for
the Canadian National Railway on maintenance crews during the summer which took him all over the island, though
he returned to Plate Cove whenever possible. Cyril is a well-
known performer around Plate Cove and was not hesitant
to share his repertoire with me. An afternoon and evening
spent with Cyril and his father playing, singing and talking
is one of my fondest memories from my stay in Plate Cove.[9]

In the summer of 1980, Mrs. Patricia (Therese) Keough
was fifty-three years old, married to Brendan Keough, with
two children, Bernard Michael and Brian. Although she does
not, as far as I know, play an instrument, she loves to dance.
She has been actively involved in many community activities,
such as the Garden Parties, and often organized and took
leading roles in the dramatic skits presented at community
concerts. She has become a liaison between a performing
group called the Red Cliff Dancers and outside agencies, such
as the St. John's Folk Arts Council, who often contact her
to invite the group to their events. Mrs. Keough's father was
from Plate Cove and his father and mother as well. Her
mother came from Tickle Cove. Therese worked away from
Plate Cove on the air base in Gander between 1947 and
1951.[10] Her husband, Brendan Keough, whom she married

in 1958, also worked in Gander at various times, though he now fishes in Plate Cove with an in-law, Jerry Tracey. Jerry lives across the lane from the Keoughs' house with his mother, Mick's sister, Mrs. Margaret (Mag) Tracey. She was born in Plate Cove East in 1900 and lived there throughout her life, raising six children alone. She played the accordion and, in her own words, loved nothing more than "music and dancing and singing and trees and flowers."[11] Mrs. Tracey played for occasional dances in Plate Cove but told me:

> I didn't make a practice of going around, just, I used to go to dances. I might take up the accordion . . . you know, and play for a part of the dance . . . .

> CQ: You must have played at home though, for yourself?

> MT: Oh my God yes. Even when the children were small. I sit down playing and they'd be singing the songs with us . . . I used to like to sit down in summertime, you know, I'd get a chair out there on the gallery [the porch] and play some tunes.[12]

Though eighty years old and suffering from arthritis, she graciously played many tunes for me and recalled the dances of her youth. Her son, Dan, and grandson, Paul, both played accordion for me as well, having learned from their mother. Mag recalled playing with Paul on her lap while he followed along with his fingers on the keys, often complaining that she went too fast.[13]

In more recent years, I was told, all the dances held in the Plate Cove School were played for by Thomas (Totty) Philpott. He and his two brothers had all died a few years before my field work, but I was able to meet his nephews, Raymond and Jim. Both play the accordion and know many of their uncle's tunes.

In the other communities nearby Plate Cove East I spoke primarily with Lloyd Oldford, the young step dancer who had so impressed me on "A Time in Red Cliff," Gerald Quinton, the harmonica player on that program, both of whom live in Red Cliff, and Larry Barker, of Open Hall, who played accordion with Gerald. Although their musical partnership is recent, Larry and Gerald have known each other for years, Larry often working for Gerald's uncle, who ran the family business. They are now often asked to play for occasions which call for the older dance music and always accompany the Red Cliff Dancers' performances.

Larry has been a public dance musician for many years and played for Garden Parties and dances "from Sweet Bay to Duntara" (see map, p.9). He learned to play from his father who also played accordion for dances and Larry performed at his first dance when he was thirteen years old. While stationed in Scotland for three years during the Second World War, Larry took lessons and learned to play a forty-bass piano-accordion which he subsequently used at dances for many years. At one time he also played the violin and he was planning to practice and relearn this instrument when I last visited him.[14]

Gerald Quinton, then fifty-six years old, has inherited the family merchant business in Red Cliff, which gives him a special status in the community. He remains somewhat of a mediator between the local people and the outside world and was very helpful to me during my research. Although he played the accordion as a young man, he was never a prominent public performer. He now prefers to play the mouth organ and often appears publicly with Larry. Gerald was once highly regarded as a step dancer and was able to show me several steps although he does not often perform now.[15]

The Plate Cove Region

As I spoke with these and other people, the social geography of this vernacular region[16] began to emerge, which should be apparent from even these few biographical comments. The four communities of Tickle Cove, Red Cliff, Open Hall, and Plate Cove East and West form a closely knit group. Summerville, formerly Indian Arm, Princeton and Sweet Bay "up" the shore and Keels, Duntara, and King's Cove "down" the shore form a larger and less cohesive region. Within the smaller group, formal and informal institutions were shared for many years. The four are always spoken of together whether one is discussing religion, schools, social events or family ties.

These four communities had all been settled by the census of 1836, though Plate Cove was clearly a new and growing community with no one over sixty and a relatively large

THE PLATE COVE REGION

BONAVISTA BAY

number of children.[17] Like other communities in Bonavista Bay, they grew from summer fishing stations into permanent settlements during the first quarter of the nineteenth century. The communities were always of mixed denominations, though either the Roman Catholics or Anglicans would dominate in any one place. Tickle Cove was mostly Catholic, Red Cliff Anglican, while Open Hall and Plate Cove were Catholic. The Roman Catholic church was centrally located in Open Hall and the Anglican in Red Cliff. Schools were built during the nineteenth century as well and, by its end, each community had one of its own dominant denomination. This remained the situation until the 1960s, when schools were consolidated.

The road system at one time ran along the shore linking each community from Plate Cove to King's Cove. Summerville, just up from Plate Cove, was less accessible because of the large ''Jigging Head'' hill which lay between the two communities. This road was largely impassable in the winter and has only recently been rerouted along the face of the cliff to reduce the grade. The old ''back road'' from Plate Cove to King's Cove eventually became the major highway. The one between Plate Cove and Open Hall has not been used since the 1950s. It is now overgrown and difficult to find, and the road which once connected Keels and Tickle Cove has been in disuse even longer.

When discussing social events with my informants, it became clear that people went back and forth between these communities frequently. Therese Keough commented that ''you knew all of 'em'' in each place. She knew Gerald and his brother, Dolph, ''ever since we were young'' and Gerald's wife, Hilda, who ''belonged to'' Open Hall, since they were all the same age. Courting was an important motive for youthful mobility. As Therese explained, ''Dolph used to go out with a girl from up here [in Plate Cove] and I used to go out with a fellow down there.''[18]

The pattern appears to be quite old. A copy of records from a King's Cove parish registry during 1825-1891 shows the great majority of marriages were between Red Cliff, Open Hall, Tickle Cove and Keels (Plate Cove was not included), while relatively few were within one community.[19]

In addition to my research in these communities I visited others more briefly and drew upon archival sources which provided a representative sample of information from throughout Newfoundland; I have indicated those communities I actually visited, those from which I was able to procure or make my own dance notation, and those from which my archive sources came, on Map 2. Although I conducted field work on the Port au Port Peninsula and in St. George's Bay, on the west coast of the island, I have chosen not to incorporate this material into this study, as the importance of French influence in these areas would have necessitated additional research beyond its scope. To demonstrate the links between socio-cultural environment and dance expression required some measure of cultural homogeneity in the region sampled. I have limited myself, therefore, to Anglo-Irish Newfoundland which, although it contains a great deal of diversity in dance as well as other cultural forms, shares many common elements.

The overwhelming majority of contemporary Newfoundlanders in the areas this study has sampled are descended from immigrants who originally came from the southwest of England and the southeast of Ireland. This population became established primarily during the first quarter of the nineteenth century and although some regional disparities persisted, there was considerable intermingling of English and Irish on the island and many mixed communities developed. By the end of the nineteenth century modern outport society had begun to take shape, and as the fishery declined after the turn of the century the outports became more introverted and isolated from the outside world. This resulted in conditions well suited to the development and preservation of a folk dance tradition.[20]

GEOGRAPHIC LOCATION OF SOURCES

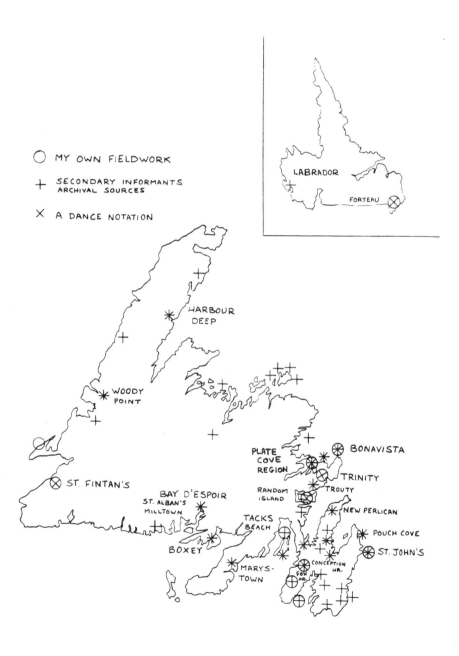

○ MY OWN FIELDWORK

+ SECONDARY INFORMANTS
   ARCHIVAL SOURCES

✕ A DANCE NOTATION

LABRADOR

FORTEAU

HARBOUR DEEP

WOODY POINT

ST. FINTAN'S

PLATE COVE REGION

BONAVISTA

TRINITY

TROUTY

RANDOM ISLAND

BAY D'ESPOIR
ST. ALBAN'S
MILLTOWN

NEW PERLICAN

TACKS BEACH

POUCH COVE

BOXEY

ST. JOHN'S

CONCEPTION HR.

FOX HR.

MARYS-TOWN

NOTES — CHAPTER 1

1. "A Time in Red Cliff," *Land and Sea*, Canadian Broadcasting Corporation, n.d.

2. The Memorial University of Newfoundland Folklore and Language Archive will be abbreviated as MUNFLA in all future references. References to my field notes, audio and video recordings are to their accession numbers, MUNFLA, 79-339 and 81-271.

3. MUNFLA, Ms., 81-271/p.245.

4. John Ashton, "Some Thoughts on the Role of Musician in Outport Newfoundland," Folklore Studies Association of Canada Meeting, Halifax, 22 May 1981.

5. MUNFLA, Ms., 81-271/pp. 8, 241.

6. MUNFLA, Ms., 81-271/p. 40.

7. MUNFLA, Ms., 81-271/p. 75.

8. MUNFLA, Ms., 81-271/pp. 76-80.

9. MUNFLA, Ms., 81-336/p. 64.

10. MUNFLA, Ms., 81-271/pp. 87-95.

11. MUNFLA, Ms., 81-271/p. 34.

12. MUNFLA, Ms., 81-271/pp. 116-17.

13. MUNFLA, Ms., 81-271/p. 183.

14. MUNFLA, Ms., 81-271/pp. 234-38.

15. MUNFLA, Ms., 81-271/pp. 176-81.

16. Gerald Pocius, "Calvert: A Study of Artifacts and Spatial Usage in a Newfoundland Community," Diss. University of Pennsylvania, 1979, pp. 48-50. Pocius discusses vernacular regions in Newfoundland.

17. *Population Returns 1836* (St. John's, 1836), n.pag.

18. MUNFLA, Ms., 81-271/p. 18.

19. Wayne Muggeridge, "A Study of the Community of Red Cliff, Bonavista Bay," Ms., in the Maritime History Group Archives, Memorial University of Newfoundland. Plate Cove was within a different parish at that time.

20. John J. Mannion, "Introduction" in *The Peopling of Newfoundland*, Memorial University of Newfoundland Social and Economic Papers, No. 8, ed. John J. Mannion (St. John's: Institute of Social and Economic Research, 1977), pp. 5, 11-12.

CHAPTER TWO: The Dances

The oldest report that I have found of a dance in Newfoundland is an 1859 newspaper advertisement for "Dancing Deportment and Calisthenics":

> Mr. A. Asch begs to announce to the ladies and gentlemen of St. John's, that he intends forming day and night classes for instruction in all the latest and most fashionable dances—namely, Valse, Mazourka, Gorlitza, La Polka, Galloppe, Guaracho, Quadrille, etc.
>
> A. Asche feels confident that after considerable practice in diff. parts of the provinces of N.S. and New Brunswick, his method of teaching need only be tried to be fully appreciated.[1]

In 1879 the *Evening Telegram* carried the following advertisement for a "Dancing School":

> Mr. Wm. Caldwell, late of Brown's Dancing Assembly, Boston, has associated himself with the talented violinist Mr. Henry Bennett, for the purpose of opening a dancing school for instruction in American plain & fancy dances.
>
> "Plain Quadrilles", "Waltz Quadrille", "Polka Quadrille", "Lancers-Quadrille", "Portland Fancy", "Chorus Jig", etc.
>
> Particular attention will be given to the "new" Schottische and the "Boston dip waltz reverse" two of the most popular dances of the day in the New England States.[2]

These two newspaper advertisements, only a sample of those that could probably be discovered, indicate that there was contact, through professional teachers, with developments in fashionable dance on the mainland even then. Whether such dances were taught in communities beyond St. John's is not documented, but certainly city fashions had some influence in the rural areas.

Judging by the evidence of the 1879 advertisement, the outports seem to have held conservatively to some of the popular dances of the late 19th century. During the first half of the 20th century these became the folk dances of Newfoundland.[3] The conservative choice of the outport dwellers is significant especially because of the accessibility, albeit minimal, of more up to date forms. Ruth Katz has made a similar point in connection with the advent of the waltz in early 19th century Europe.[4] Although whirling couple dances had long been in the folk repertoire, they swept the European ballrooms when they suddenly became compatible with changed social conditions. In a parallel way, though "modern" dances were always accessible, a relatively small and homogeneous repertoire of 19th century-derived folk dances was the overwhelming choice of outport Newfoundlanders until quite recently.

My primary focus has been this older repertoire of dances which had many years of use in a relatively stable, conservative social environment during which time they were transmitted in a traditional manner and developed traditional versions. It is primarily in relation to this historical background that I will discuss the newer popular dance forms, disseminated and validated in large part by the mass media, which have now largely replaced the older repertoire. My findings show that the recent changes in Newfoundland dance, although often perceived as an abrupt abandonment of the older forms, are only one aspect of a reordering of the entire configuration of behaviour which is Newfoundland dance culture. Within this expressive system, there have been many continuities as well as changes throughout the span of living memory.

A large number of dances are considered vernacular by Newfoundlanders. These include the widely reported Square Dance, Lancers, and Step Dance, and less well documented dances such as the Reel, Sir Roger, and the Kissing Dance, and others which were merely mentioned in my archival sources.[5] Previous descriptions of most are inadequate for detailed analysis, but enough information is usually available to classify their organization as individual, mixed-sex couple, or group, in form.

The structure of the dances is tied to that of the music. In common with British/North American traditions generally, the dance tunes usually have two strains of equal length, each played twice in performance. They are generally in duple meter and may be compound or simple time, predominantly in 2/4, 4/4, and 6/8 meters. Individual dance movement is performed in synchrony with the beat and basic structural units are ideally synchronized with the melodic phrases.

Rhythm may be important to distinctions made among dances. The Step Dance for example has several forms distinguished by meter and tempo. Different parts within the group dances are often distinguished by characteristic meters and tempos. Musicians also make general distinctions among dance tunes based on their rhythm using descriptive terms such as "single," "double," and "triple." Cyril Keough, for example, described my playing of Soldier's Joy as "double," but demonstrated how one could "play he single" as well. The double used sixteenth notes, the single only eighth note divisions of the quarter note beat.[6]

Some tunes used to accompany the Step Dance may often be identified as "triples." Many people, however, refer to the Step Dance as the "Double," and the tunes which are used to accompany it, by extension, as "double tunes." This paradoxical usage of "triple" and "double" probably derives from a confusion of two descriptive systems, one for music and the other for dance steps, which both use the term "double."

Among my Harbour Buffett informants, single tunes are played in duple simple times and usually subdivide a quarter note beat into eighth notes, occasionally using sixteenth notes as rhythmic ornament. They are generally played at about ♩ = MM152. Double tunes, in this system, are played in duple compound time using either a 6/8 |♩♪♩♪| or 6/8 |♫♫ ♫♫| rhythm, at ♩. = MM160. Triple tunes are again in duple simple time, but they employ predominantly sixteenth note divisions of the beat, and are played at ♩ =MM 132, a slightly slower tempo. As dance accompaniment, however, they required faster footwork of the dancer to beat out the sixteenth note rhythms.[7]

Other musicians I spoke with had no name for the 6/8 rhythm although they used it frequently. Whether identified by vernacular terms or not, these three rhythms, apart from the waltz, are those most used to accompany traditional dancing.

Particular tunes were favored for different dances or parts of dances. Although structurally interchangeable, tunes in the same meter may have different rhythmic qualities, and so might be better suited to some dance movements than others. Mrs. Tracey commented frequently on this aspect of tunes. After playing a version of ''The Rose Tree,'' which she knew as ''Curly Buck,'' she commented it was good for the first part of a Square Dance. She added that another part of the dance,

> ''Form a line,'' calls for a slowish one . . . [while] the last bar, ''ladies in,'' you don't always have a real jig tune. But you can have it if you like, if people can dance. There's a lot of swinging in the last part in the last bar of the dance and cutting about.[8]

Gerald Quinton described the music he and Larry Barker play as ''fast,'' explaining that the dancers ''liked it better that way. It gives the dancing more life.''[9] Their music has a driving, insistent rhythm, which is accented by the loud foot tapping both use to accompany their playing. As an informant from Conception Bay noted,

> Usually the fiddler or accordion player walked with a slight roll or limp since the heel of the right foot was usually worn down lower than the left.[10]

One assumes this was the result of energetic foot tapping as the musician ''gave it to her.''

Floor plans are also significant. While the individual Step Dance is performed basically in one spot, and the couple dances are relatively free of floor plan elaboration, among the group dances floor plans are intricate, prescribed and the most important basis for distinguishing one dance from another. Distinctions between floor plans are also common in the vernacular terminology employed by informants to describe and discuss their dances. The elaboration of names for floor plan movements in the dances, along with the distinctions made between dances on this basis, reflect the importance of spatial design in the tradition. The vernacular terms may be applied flexibly, but reflect in general the hierarchical organization of movement units in the dances. In describing a group dance such as the Square Dance, for example, informants usually gave the name of the whole dance, which identifies its organization. They then divided this into parts, or ''bars,'' named for a particular floor design, each of which consisted of several "steps," or "moves," by which was meant a smaller movement sequence. Step dancing is also composed of "steps," which are short sequences of foot tapping which the dancer combines when performing. A problem for the researcher is the application of many different names to similar dance patterns, and the same names to different patterns. Such confusion in terminology is probably due to the lack of occasion for verbalization about the tradition. As long as dancers knew what to do, and the musicians knew what to play, which was usually learned primarily by observation and imitation, there was little need for a systematic descriptive terminology. The welter of diversity in terminology and practice found in Newfoundland is typical of living folk traditions, in which performers adapt and invent forms in a creative expressive process.[11]

Aesthetic Norms

Underlying the diversity of design and rhythm in the Newfoundland dances is a characteristic use of the body. Dancers generally perform in an upright posture with little torso movement. Movement articulation is primarily in the legs and feet, with which the dancers perform complex stepping, tapping out the musical rhythms with their heels and toes. The feet are, nonetheless, usually kept directly under the body. The arms and hands hang naturally at the dancer's sides or may be slightly raised with a flexed elbow. Arm and hand gestures are not considered a significant part of the dance, and too much movement of them is usually thought to detract from the performance.

An interesting application of these norms can be seen in the construction of the "dancing dolls" sometimes found in Newfoundland, as well as elsewhere in North America. These use one block of wood for the torso, to which are attached legs and arms which freely swing. The doll is held by a stick placed in its back and bounced on a springy board, in time with a dance tune, to create a droll image of a dancing man.[12]

The most admired step dancers were the "tidiest," and those who did not move all over the floor. Even in a step such as the "side step," which called for the dancer to move, or "cut," across the floor, the footwork should still be "neat," and kept directly under the body. In addition to neatness, "lightness" was also much admired. These standards may be illustrated by the observation that some of the old people were so light on their feet they could dance on a tin, or enamel pan, turned bottom up on the floor.[13] Short anecdotes of dancing on plates have been reported throughout Newfoundland. I recorded one story of a man from Sally's Cove, on the West Coast, who could dance with a glass of water on his head without spilling a drop.[14] Herbert Halpert has recorded the expression, "so-and-so could dance on a tea plate," to indicate lightness on one's feet and the ability to dance without moving from a given spot.[15] Another man described this ability by claiming he could dance on a "thole pin," the wooden peg used as an oarlock.[16] One informant of mine commented that his father, a step dancer from Bonavista, could dance on a two-by-four if need be.[17]

These stories are apparently based on traditional step dancing feats performed by good dancers. A professed eyewitness of a plate-dancing performance in Newfoundland described it as "something like a [Scottish] sword dance" in which the performer danced around and over the plate, turned bottom up on the floor, occasionally touching it with his toe or heel.[18] The dancer did not "plank 'er down," i.e. stamp heavily, right on the plate, a physical impossibility, but contrived to make it seem that he was dancing "on" the plate. If nothing else, he demonstrated tremendous control of his movements and the same skills described by informants as neatness and lightness, which were required for good dancing. Such feats formed the basis for narratives which were used to illustrate these same qualities. These folk narratives are traditional statements of aesthetic standards within the tradition, and are known in other parts of North America and the British Isles.[19]

Such standards are also implied in conventional phrases such as "close to the floor," which one hears as a shout of encouragement or in requests for a certain type of performance. Dancers, as well as being light and neat, are expected to keep their movements small and subtle. The high kicking clog dance style of the Southern Appalachians would not be acceptable in Newfoundland.[20]

The upright postural norm is also implied in descriptions of comic dancing which I heard. Such dancers, often "half shot," would get themselves "in all kinds of shapes" and "did everything in the world" with their body. It is the upright norm which makes such movements incorrect and humorous.[21]

These standards apply to individuals performing in the group dances as well, and although special segments of these dances were designated as times for the men to "dance," i.e. step dance, attention was paid to footwork throughout the performance. According to Cyril Keough and Mrs. Tracey:

> The old people, they never wanted to miss a beat. Could dance forward or backstep right with the music and never wanted to be off. Now the scattered one that didn't have an ear might make the big stamp when 'twas only half over [the musical phrase or dance step] and they might put you out![22]

While a range of individual variation from these norms is typical, there is a pervasive contrast between male and female dance practice. In general, men take a more active role and perform energetic stepping throughout the group dances, while the women may simply stand in place.[23] Neither do women often perform the solo Step Dance. When women do step dance they perform similarly to the men. While men were expected to be able to dance, "it was sort of a bonus if a woman was an especially good dancer." The woman from Port de Grave, Conception Bay, of whom that was said, was highly regarded because "she could sing, dance, and play as well as any man."[24]

Step Dancing

Step Dancing is performed in the context of the group dances, but it is also found as a distinct form in itself. The Step Dance at its most formal is a solo performance for an audience. It may also take the form of a competition between two dancers or a freely organized group of dancers all stepping together.

21

According to oral tradition, in Port Kirwan on the Southern Shore, the Double, a solo step dance with thirty-two steps, was introduced in the mid-nineteenth century by an Irish school master, William O'Neill. He taught the dance to a few men and it was transmitted to at least two performers who are still living.[25] Similarly, single, double and treble hornpipes once performed in St. Brendan's, Bonavista Bay, can be traced to an Irish immigrant who was known as a "Professor of Dance."[26]

The "hornpipe" is rarely mentioned as a solo dance form in Newfoundland.[27] Descriptions of this dance from Ireland however indicate that it was much like the Newfoundland Double. According to Breandán Breathnach, for example, the hornpipe dance in Ireland was

> usually danced by one man alone. It was rarely danced by a woman as the steps were regarded as requiring the vigor and sound which only a man could bring to them.[28]

J.G. O'Keefe comments that

> when danced by two [the hornpipe] . . . assumes the character of a friendly contest, each man dancing his steps in turn, one resting while the other is dancing.[29]

Music for the Irish hornpipe is in duple simple meter, and similar to a reel, "but it is played in a more deliberate manner, with a well defined accent on the first and third beats of each bar."[30] While the term hornpipe is not often applied to dance music in Newfoundland, there is enough evidence to conclude that the Double is derived from the Irish hornpipe. In Newfoundland, however, it is performed at a brisker tempo.

While most men in a community could probably dance a few steps, specialized skill in dancing, as with many other performance genres, belonged to particular individuals. Certain families likewise became well known for their dancing skill. Good dancers can often identify the men they tried to emulate and children were sometimes more formally taught to step dance. One student recalled that he stood between two chairs, supported himself on their backs, and danced while someone sang the following verse:

> Go to ged, go to bed, go to bed Tom
> Get up in the morning and beat your drum

When your drum is beat and your work is done
Go to bed, go to bed, go to bed Tom.

This procedure was thought to be useful in gaining equal coordination of both legs which was "one of the basic requirements of a good step dancer."[31] Most step dancers, however, seem to have learned by observation and subsequent private practice. One man, for example, recalled that he taught himself by dancing on the wooden floor in the cow barn, while playing his own accompaniment on the mouth organ.[32]

The characteristic use of the body described earlier applies generally to the Step Dance, but there is a great deal of individual and probably regional variety in performance style as well. Styles may be differentiated by small differences in body stance, arm use, or characteristic ways of using the feet. Dancers of the previous generation in Harbour Buffett, Placentia Bay, for example, strove to achieve a light and nearly silent dance style. Later on the sound of the rhythm danced became much more important, and many of the younger dancers sacrificed lightness for volume. The older generation of Harbour Buffett also felt that a good dancer should move only from the knees down.[33] In contrast, a recorded performance by Johnny Power at the 1977 "Good Entertainment" festival shows increasing animation during the dance as he swings and raises his arms freely, claps, and begins to move about the floor.[34]

Breaking out of the typical body attitude maintained during almost all dancing is a technique used sparingly during step dance performances to accent a movement and create excitement. Lloyd Oldford, for example, will often swing one leg up from the hip, keeping his knee straight, clap his hands under it and then stamp loudly to accent the end of musical phrases. A highlight of every dance in the Dock, Conception Bay, was reported to be a "tap" (i.e. step) dance performance by a man who did the final steps on his knees.[35] I have seen and heard of other dancers who would drop to their knees during some of their steps. The audience responds with surprised incredulity. The dancer is down on his knees and back up without losing the beat, almost before one realizes what has happened. Such striking visual and auditory changes are used to accent the dance and are experienced as particularly exciting.

Gerald Quinton is known around Red Cliff as an accomplished step dancer. At one time, he told me he knew nineteen of the twenty-two steps for the Double. In Port Kirwan, it was ascribed thirty-two steps, as was the "treble hornpipe" in St. Brendan's, and the Sailor's Hornpipe in the Dock, Conception Bay.[36] Gerald reported, similarly to other reports of the Step Dance, that he performed most often at large dance events in between the group dances. He usually danced alone in this context and felt that when more than one dancer got up on the floor it detracted from the performance, which would become confused. When performing, Gerald would begin with the easier steps and progress to the more complicated, which were usually those that sounded more subdivisions of the beat. In one series of steps for the Double which he showed me, though each sounded the same beats, there was an increase in the amount of movement in each and thus of energy conveyed by their performance. In the final steps of the series, the dancer is constantly springing slightly into the air as he changes his weight from foot to foot. The good dancer will not spring very far off the ground and the motion may not even be perceptible to the viewer, yet the dancer's weight will, in fact, be off the ground much of the time, which is perceived as the quality traditionally termed "lightness."[37]

Formal structuring of steps used in the dance is commonly mentioned by step dancers, but I have rarely seen it in practice. A dancer from Bonavista who now lives in St. John's and performs both formally and informally, described his use of steps as follows:

> I use both my legs the same, eh. The way I mostly dance is, like say, "Mussels in the Corner" eh, I do one line, swinging one leg, eh, and then the next line I do it on the other leg, same thing. Then the next line I change it, do another step 'til I come back to the first one again. And then the third time I do a different step again and come back to the first one again; always come back to the first.[38]

Gerald likewise considered the ability to use both feet alike

24

one of the more difficult skills required of a good dancer. Changing performance contexts and a declining knowledge of dance among the potential audience may have eroded a once more highly structured form. Or there may always have been a gap between the acknowledged ideal and practice.

While step dancing in Newfoundland is similar to Irish traditions in the dance techniques used and the terminology applied to both dance and music, both are regional expressions of a tradition known widely in Britain and North America. In their study of *Traditional Step-Dancing in Lakeland* J.F. and T.M. Flett have identified two major types which were widespread in England within living memory.[39] Elements of both can be seen in Newfoundland as well. The first type consists of improvised movements which are not codified or systematized in any way. I saw several such performances during my stay in Plate Cove. These dancers, however, move within the aesthetic parameters of the tradition, and if one were to record enough of their dancing, a few basic movements would probably be found repeated in different combinations. The second type of step dancing consists of set sequences, systematically constructed from a number of basic movements. The style of movement within this type may be either compact, with emphasis on the sound of the dancing, or much more expansive, with an emphasis on the visual effect of the step. The first style, the Fletts believe, originated in crowded pub settings, the second almost certainly on stage, probably during the eighteenth century.

Both of these dance movement styles can be seen in Newfoundland as well. In general, however, the "closer" style seems to predominate. Step dancing in stage-like performance contexts such as the hall times, however, has encouraged the use of visual effects within the bounds of the traditional aesthetic, and more recent stage adaptation has begun to assert a new influence on this dance form.

Several miscellaneous dance titles seem to refer to particular types of step dance. The Monkey Dance, for example, was described to me as a step in which one would squat on the floor and kick his legs out alternately. "You've seen the Russians do it," it was explained.[40] This dance movement is a part of British tradition as well, however. Cecil Sharp reports the Monkey or Kibby dance from Somerset and Devon in which the performer crouched on his haunches alternately throwing forward his legs.[41] A now well-known illustration from the tenth century, reproduced by Joseph Strutt, shows two Saxon glee men performing a dance in this squatting position. Strutt comments, writing in 1801, that, ''attitudes somewhat similar I have seen occur in some of the steps of a modern hornpipe.''[42] Breathnach describes the very similar Irish Frog Dance, or Cobbler's Dance.[43]

''Cover the Buckle'' is another dance title which I have occasionally come across, but which is seldom described. According to one source:

> This was done by dancing around and over a broom, which was placed on the floor, without touching it and required great agility.[44]

These miscellaneous step dances are similar to the extraordinary feats discussed earlier, such as dancing on a plate, small surface, or balancing a glass of water on one's head while performing. Such exhibitions border on other types of physical contest and challenge in which young men often engaged.[45]

Step dancing generally in Newfoundland is improvisatory. Although it originates in a tradition influenced by the formalization introduced by dancing masters, in Newfoundland it has been primarily informal. Performances are found in individual, dual-competitive, or free group organizations. It provides a framework for the elaboration of individual dance movement and its aesthetic standards permeate all forms of traditional dancing.

Couple Dances

Mixed-sex couple dancing outside the framework of the group dances was not commonly reported in my sources. The Waltz was mentioned most often but its performance was never described, beyond the comment that in some places it was ''competitive.''[46]

In my own dancing I found the ''old fashioned waltz,'' as my dancing partners called it, to be a fairly typical folk waltz in 3/4 meter. Occasionally, however, I heard other slow couple dances called waltzes regardless of their rhythm. In the usual closed position, dancers start moving to the man's left with a large step to the side on the count of one, slide the other foot closed on two, and change weight briefly on three, beginning again with the opposite foot on one. Couples rotate clockwise and travel more or less counter clockwise around the room while dancing.[47]

The Polka was mentioned a few times in my sources, but with no description. As I danced it in Branch, it was a whirling couple dance in which couples in closed position started to the man's left with a small leap onto that foot, followed by a hop on the same foot, then a leap onto the other foot, followed by a hop, and so forth. Legs could be kicked back from the knees when unweighted. Combined with a clockwise whirling motion and counter clockwise traveling around the room, this resulted in a minimum of control over one's movements and frequent collisions with the other dancers.[48]

Couples were reported as occasionally step dancing with one another to the sides of a room during group dances. This was not very frequently mentioned however, and always in passing. It was not, apparently, considered a distinctive dance form.

The lack of emphasis given these forms is important, as both the Waltz and Polka were popular during the nineteenth century, along with the group dances which came to predominate in Newfoundland. From the historical evidence it appears that couple forms were known but not practised to a significant extent.

Group Dances

The group dances form the most numerous category of Newfoundland folk dance and they include several formations of which the square dances are the most widely known. These include the Square Dance, Lancers, Reel, and the Cotillion. Longways dances have also been reported, as well as many often pantomimic dance games. Of these latter, the Kissing Dance was well known in the Plate Cove area.

The floor pattern and the directions followed by individual dancers are the most clearly conceived and highly articulated aspects of the group dances. They constitute a prescribed framework within which dancers improvise steps. In traveling movements, the dancers use a "dance walk," in which the weight is kept well forward. The dancers are free to vary this with more complex footwork if they are not traveling during the entire phrase of music available for the movement. This dancing is similar to the individual step dance. Male dancers in general do more of this improvising. While stationary, the performers continue to "dance" in this fashion. The men who could keep this up with undiminished vigour through the whole dance were often considered the best dancers.[49] This individualistic stepping is characterized by an emphasis on the final beat of the musical phrase. Lloyd Oldford, for instance, will often mark this beat with a small jump onto both feet, or a loud stamp. During the step dance sequences in the Square Dance, Lloyd will perform more complex steps, perhaps building to an exciting climax of hand clapping, high leg kicks, and stamping to conclude the phrase. In general practice, I have never seen dancing perfectly phrased with the music, although "keeping time" was frequently upheld as a mark of good dancing.[50] Each dance performance would be unique, depending upon the skill of the individual dancers and musicians, their mood, and the social context.

The Square Dance

The dance most commonly mentioned during my research was the Square Dance. While this name has been used in many ways, in Newfoundland it refers to a particular dance, derived from the 19th century quadrilles. It is usually performed in a square formation, couples facing from one side to another, and has several distinct parts. The pairs of facing couples dance with one another, and all together, moving through different prescribed floor designs.

How it came to be known as the Square Dance is not clear. In the United States and mainland Canada, the term is often used in a generic sense, indicating a whole class of dances using this form. Discussing dances in Kentucky, Burt Feintuch, for example, uses the term to refer to modern derivations of such "square" dances which are performed in circle formations, as well as the social events at which these dances take place.[51] Influence from the mainland during the Second World War may have encouraged the use of this term in Newfoundland. As there is evidence of decreasing diversity since the nineteenth century in square dances, it may be that this generic term came to apply to the progressively standardized form which survived. In Newfoundland today, while "square dance" is used as a generic term, it most commonly refers to a specific dance. These vary from place to place, but a comparison of these variants shows them to be versions of the same dance type.

I have never seen the entire Square Dance successfully performed as a purely "social" (as contrasted with "presentational") dance, but I have seen fragments which can be identified in the original from which they are taken. Based on a videotape recording of the dance as taught by the Red Cliff Dancers, observations at other performances, and interviews with the performers and others from their communities, I have reconstructed the Square Dance as formerly performed in the Plate Cove area.[52]

My description of the Square Dance is based on those of my informants. Their descriptions of the dance indicate how the dancers perceive its component movement sequences, and provide a vocabulary with which to identify these parts. For convenience I have also employed certain commonly used terms in my discussion of the dance figures which are not used by my informants, but rather are derived from the "how to" literature of the folk dance revival. They are specific in meaning, not difficult to understand, and make the descriptions considerably less verbose.

The "set" is the formation in which dancers begin the dance, within which and in relation to which they move. In the Square Dance, this is a square made up of pairs of couples facing one another from opposite sides. One pair of sides is labelled "ends," the other "sides," and the couples in them end- and side-couples, respectively. The term "corners" refers to the couples which may occasionally be formed between the end- and side-couples at the corners of the square set. I will often describe floor patterns in terms of this square set. Dancers may cross from one side to the other or be "in the center." Each couple starts the dance in their "home place," or position in the set, and dancers may, for example, "return to place," from another position. The pairs of facing couples may be called opposites, and to distinguish the couples of a facing pair, one is labelled first, the other second. Descriptions such as "first man swings the second woman" are thus possible.

As performed by the Red Cliff Dancers the Square Dance consists of five parts, or "bars," which are performed by both the end and side pairs of facing couples. These bars are separated one from another by a break in the musical accompaniment which would last long enough in the traditional performing context to allow both dancers and musician a brief rest. While there is some variation in terminology, the first four bars are generally agreed to be as follows: (1) "off she goes" (2) "dance up" (3) "form a line" and, (4) "take two." As currently performed the fifth bar is called the "grand cut." An alternate fifth bar, the "ladies in," is also known in the Plate Cove region and was apparently more popular in former years. An additional, optional bar, "thread the needle," could be added if desired.

I have identified each movement pattern in the dance by a term which indicates one of several basic movement possibilities. Within the square formation, dancers may cross the set, meet in the center, step dance more or less in place, swing with another dancer, or travel around the set. These basic floor pattern movements are performed in a variety of ways by different dancers and combined to create different designs. For example, dancers may cross the set as individuals, or as couples, holding hands, or in a closed "social dance" position. They may return immediately or after some other movement sequence. Couples may swing either clockwise (the usual direction) or counterclockwise, using a variety of holds. When performers step dance during the performance, they do so without a prescribed floor plan to follow. The movement is ideally considered to take place on one spot, though in practice dancers may move about somewhat, usually towards the center of the set.

At the lowest structural level of significant dance movement are the basic movements I have identified as "cross," "meet," "step dance," "swing" and "circle," each of which is closely phrased with the music in performance. These basic movements may also be combined into longer movement sequences, which form minor units in the dance.

Minor movement units are of several types: individual, couple, and group interactions. The basic movements are combined within these organizational forms to create the different figures of the dance. The figures in turn are subsumed within the bar divisions, which together make up the entire dance.

There are some rules for combining the basic movements and minor units in sequence. All sequences eventually return the dancers to the position from which they began. If someone crosses the set, they will eventually cross back. Furthermore, any movements which are performed by the dancers in one couple of the facing pair will eventually be repeated by the others. These design principles result in a symmetry which runs through the entire structure of the dance, except for the bar divisions which progress, each one different from the others.

While all the bars contain the same basic movements as minor units, each also contains a unique movement design which I have called its "distinctive figure."[53] This distinctive figure often gives its name to the entire bar, as in "form a line" and "take two." "Dance up" appears to be a title for the distinctive use of the basic meeting movement which begins and repeats throughout this bar. "Off she goes" is, apparently, simply a reference to the beginning of the dance. The final bar is usually named for the "grand cut," but has also been referred to by titles taken from other figures within it, such as the "round the house."

The other minor units, found throughout the dance, I have termed secondary figures. These may precede or follow the distinctive figure in a bar and also occur between the symmetrical repetitions of distinctive figures.

The duration of the basic movements, and some minor units, is flexible. While unintentional variations occur when dancers become confused or forget the next movement, intentional variation is more significant. Gerald Quinton, in an interpretation of the term "double," commented on this practice as follows:

> See, they call out "double it up" in a square dance after
> so long and they want to dance the same step over
> again.[54]

In this instance, the term "step" seems to refer to a minor
unit in the dance. In this way, a spin or step dance sequence
could be lengthened or shortened if the dancers wished.

The first four bars are performed alternately by the end
and side couples. In the first, "off she goes," the facing
couples cross the set as individuals, the women changing
places first, and then return similarly to place. Once back
the men step dance vigorously, the women less so, and partners swing in place. This is followed by a pattern I call the
"ladies' chain" in which the women cross the set, swing
counter clockwise with the opposite man and return to place.
The opposite couples then dance forward and back, meeting
in the center, step dance, and swing.

In "dance up," the second bar, facing couples meet in
the center and step dance. The couples cross the set, meet,
and step dance again. This sequence is repeated once more
to return the couples to place, and the bar ends with partners swinging in place.

In the distinctive figure of "form a line" the first man
turns the second woman by the left hand once around in
the center and both join right hands with their partners to
form a linked line of four dancers. The dancers step dance
in this position. The first man and second woman move from
the center to her side of the set, while the second man crosses
to join the first woman on her side. Having exchanged partners, these couples meet in the center, step dance, and swing.
The men then cross back to their own side, and repeat the
couples meet, step dance, and swing sequence. This entire
pattern is repeated for the second man and first woman.

"Take two" begins with the minor "ladies' chain" movement also found in "off she goes." The distinctive figure
follows, in which the first woman crosses to stand on the
second man's left, forming a group of three who put their
arms around each others' backs. The first man, now alone,
performs an especially vigorous step dance. The second couple crosses to the opposite side and the first man joins his

partner in the second couple's place, and both step dance. The couples then cross back to place, step dance, and swing. The entire sequence, including the "ladies' chain" is repeated, the couples reversing roles.

To begin the fifth bar, "grand cut," all the dancers, both end and side couples, join together in a ring and step dance. The ring circles clockwise, once around. The distinctive "grand cut" figure follows in which the set separates again into couples, each in their original place and the end couples side step (i.e. "cut") across the set and back to place, in closed position, twice, swing, and perform the "ladies' chain" sequence. This much is repeated from the beginning, the side couples performing the "grand cut" this time. The bar then continues with an exchange partners figure which begins with the join together and step dance movement. Corners then swing and form new couples which perform the distinctive "off she goes" figure, end couples first. This sequence is repeated, exchanging partners each time, until the original couples are reunited. The dance concludes with two "join together," step dance, and circle sequences (first left, then right), and a final all step dance and partners swing.

The alternate distinctive fifth bar figure, "ladies in," is performed as follows. The women meet in the center and step dance, then return to place. Couples dance counterclockwise around the perimeter of the set and exchange partners, women moving to the next man clockwise around the set (i.e. behind them). The sequence is repeated until original partners are reunited.

Following either the "grand cut," or "ladies in," "thread the needle" could be performed. In this bar the dancers join together in a ring and circle to the left. The first man lets go the hand of the woman on his left and moving into the center leads the line now following him under the upraised arms of his partner and the man to her right. The first man continues on around behind his partner and back into the center again to lead the line of dancers under the next arch, that between the next couple to his right in the set. He continues in this manner, passing between each pair of dancers. The last woman may lead the set to her right around the circle. This will increase the speed of the movement and accentuate its spiral design. The first man may turn immediately under his own arm to start if he wishes. Each man in turn leads the figure.

The formation, organization, and basic movements of the Square Dance are typical of 19th century quadrilles. While I have not attempted to trace the historical provenance of this variant, its origin may clearly be seen in even the earliest description available to me, the "First Set" of Quadrilles introduced to English Ballrooms from Paris in 1815.[55]

The most striking similarities are found in several distinctive figures which are easily recognized. The third part of this quadrille includes the four-in-line formation and the fourth part contains this familiar pattern:

> A gentleman and his partner present hands, then advance and retire twice, leaving hands at the second time; the lady going off, places herself to the left of the gentleman opposite, returns and retires backwards. The opposite gentleman, who is then between two ladies, gives a hand to each of them, and all three advance and retire twice . . . . The remaining gentleman, who is left alone, then advances in this turn twice also.[56]

The style of dancing, music, and performance context of the dance have undergone many changes since that description was written in 1830. The genetic connection is clear, however, and, significantly, is most obvious in the structure and distinctive minor units.

Different regional versions of the Newfoundland Square Dance are similarly consistent in structure and distinctive figures, although the secondary figures used and their position in the dance are often quite different. Versions of the Square Dance may be identified as such by their structure and common distinctive figures. Many variants of this dance have been reported from elsewhere in Newfoundland, and, despite many differences, these aspects of the dance remain recognizably the same.

The Square Dance Chart in Table 1 summarizes a comparison among seven versions of the Square Dance reported from different areas of Newfoundland.[57] The distinctive figure of each bar is identified by a verbal shorthand which indicates the basic movement or formation it employs. The

TABLE 1

DISTINCTIVE FIGURES OF THE SQUARE DANCE

Red Cliff/Plate Cove. B.B.	cross singly	couples cross	Form a line	Take two		join together (couples cross) exchange partners	join together (optional)	
Stock Cove. B.B.	cross singly	couples cross	Form a line	Take two		join together	exchange partners	
New Perlican. T.B.	couples cross	couples cross	Form a line	Take two		join together	exchange partners	
Trouty. T.B.	cross singly	couples cross	Form a line	Take two	couples cross	join together	exchange partners	
Port de Grave. C.B.	cross singly	couples cross	Form a line	Take two	couples cross	exchange partners		
Tack's Beach. P.B.	couples cross		Take two	Form a line	couples cross	join together	exchange partners	
Bay d'Espoir	women cross	couples cross	Swing one	Take two		exchange partners	join partners	
Forteau	women cross singly	couples cross	swing one	Take two	couples cross	join together	exchange partners	join together (optional)

35

bar divisions, marked by interruptions of the musical accompaniment, are indicated by vertical lines. The dance is also divided into structural sections, indicated at the bottom of the chart, which apply to all the noted versions.

From a comparative analysis of regional variants a conceptual model of the underlying dance form emerges. The opening bar or two involves the facing couples crossing the set. The next two or three bars contain the more complex facing couple interactions of ''form a line'' and ''take two.'' The latter portion of the dance includes two types of distinctive figures performed by all the dancers, occasionally reversed or combined, the ''join together'' and ''exchange partners'' patterns. Each bar, with its distinctive figure, is subject to forms of elaboration and abridgement by secondary figures, which may be interpolated at various points.

The initial crossing figures usually take up two bars, as in the Red Cliff/Plate Cove version. The first involves couples crossing the set separately as individuals, the second, as couples. The ''cross singly'' figures may involve both men and women or just women, as in ladies' chain figures. The ''couples cross'' figures may require the dancers to simply ''pass by'' each other or ''go under'' one couple's linked arms. Performed in conjunction with these patterns are secondary step dancing, meeting and swinging, which are interpolated at various points in the distinctive crossing figures. There is close agreement among the different versions of the third and fourth bars of the Red Cliff/Plate Cove dance, ''form a line'' and ''take two.'' All save two contain the same distinctive ''four-in-line'' and ''take two women'' patterns. As in the first two bars, each dance version combines the distinctive figure with characteristic secondary movement patterns.

Figures in the final section of the Square Dance are danced by both groups of facing couples together. Several figures are commonly found, of two basic types: the ''join together'' movements in which dancers join hands to form a ring, which may include all the dancers or just the men or women; and, the ''exchange partners'' movements in which each man and woman dances with all those of the opposite sex. The final bars of the Square Dance often include one or more of these figures in a variety of combinations. My informants from Plate Cove, for example, recalled using the join together figures, "ladies in," and "close in," as well as "right and left," an exchange partners figure, which might, optionally, be followed by a final join together of "thread the needle". "Round the house" is another common exchange partners movement, in which couples dance around the set. Secondary facing couple figures may also be interpolated into the final section, as is the "cutting" across the set found in the Red Cliff Dancers' performance.

While structural formulas for each version could be constructed (building up from the basic movements to the bar divisions), these would, I think, be more confusing than helpful in conceptualizing the structural form of the Square Dance. Instead, I will summarize the constant structural framework and levels of variation.

All these versions of the Square Dance share a progressive sequence of distinctive figures, moving from simple to more complex facing couple interactions and culminating in several figures for all the dancers together. The distinctive figures remain relatively constant, while they are embellished with secondary figures which characterize the different regional versions. Where the Red Cliff dancers employ the "ladies' chain and spin" sequence, for example, the New Perlican dancers perform "change partners and swing," a variation of the same facing couple interaction. In the Trouty version there is a similar secondary figure, while the other versions do not use this minor movement unit sequence at all. The distinctive figures may also be elaborated by manoeuvering couples into crossed positions in the set. They must then return to place which provides another opportunity to interpolate a secondary step dance or spin movement.

In all these versions, as well, the dancers are divided into two groups of facing couples who perform the figures alternately. The alternation may occur halfway through the distinctive figure as in the Tack's Beach version, or, more commonly, after the entire bar sequence has been completed. In one version I collected in the Bay St. George region, the side couples have been eliminated completely and the facing couple figures were performed without interruption by one group of facing couples. This form retains the basic sequence of distinctive figures, but eliminates its repetition and streamlines the dance considerably. In some places, one large set would accommodate all the dancers, as in the Plate Cove region, but elsewhere, as in Tack's Beach, several small sets, each with their own end and side couples, would perform simultaneously.

Throughout all the variations in vernacular terminology, organization, and movement sequences, the Square Dance retains its identity as a group dance consisting of a prescribed sequence of distinctive figures, performed by couples in pairs and all together. Within this framework regional variation occurs in the organization of these parts and the secondary movement units. Individual variation and improvisation is found in steps and embellishments of the basic movements, such as idiosyncratic ways of swinging. The entire dance performance takes the dancers from a home position as a couple, moves them through a known sequence of figures in which they interact with each other in a variety of ways and returns them, at the end, home again with their partners.

The Lancers

Although fewer descriptions of the Lancers are available than of the Square Dance, it was certainly widely known and is mentioned in sources from most areas of the Province. It is organized similarly to the Square Dance, though performed only in four couple sets. Like the Square Dance, it consists of several major sections, each usually containing its own distinctive figure, with which secondary figures are incorporated.

Table 2 provides a comparative chart of three variants of the Lancers, recorded in Trinity, Trinity Bay, Pouch Cove, and Conception Harbour, Conception Bay.[58] As in Table 1 each distinctive figure is identified and interruptions in the musical accompaniment are indicated by vertical lines.

Similarly to the Square Dance, the Lancers begins with crossing figures for the facing couples. As I saw the dance performed in Trinity, opposite couples dance forward and back, then cross over the set, one couple forming an arch.

TABLE 2

DISTINCTIVE FIGURES OF THE LANCERS

Trinity	couples cross	women cross	star	basket	longways reel	exchange partners (right and left)	
Pouch Cove	couples cross	women cross	join together	longways reel	basket	star	exchange partners (right and left)	join together (thread the needle)
Conception Harbour	couples meet	women cross	basket	star	longways reel	exchange partners right and left	join together (thread the needle)

The couples swing in the opposite place and return in like manner, the other couple arching. Both couples then swing. The side couples then perform this sequence. The first figure done in Pouch Cove has the same cross over arching movement found in Trinity, but without the swing in opposite place. All then swing their corners upon returning to place. In the Lancers, as performed in Conception Harbour, the facing couples dance forward and back, swing their opposites, and return to swing their corners. The side couples do this and the whole is then repeated.

The second part of the Lancers is much the same in all three versions. Head couples dance forward and back and forward again, the women exchanging places and returning with the opposite men. These movements are repeated to bring the women back home. In Conception Harbour, both head and side couples do this twice, as in the first part. In Trinity, the couples bow after exchanging partners and then swing corners before repeating the movement to home place. The Pouch Cove Lancers is somewhat elaborated in this part. After exchanging partners, lines are formed by splitting the set through the side couples. The lines dance forward and back twice, then form rings and circle in both directions. They dance forward and back twice again, taking their partners to swing and return home upon the second meeting. The side couples then repeat the entire figure, the lines formed by splitting the head couples this time.

The central portion of the Lancers, as can be seen from Table 2, consists of three distinctive figures: the "star", "basket," and "progressive longways." Though they may appear in a different order, the figures themselves are much the same in each dance. To form the "star," men join right hands with the opposite man, putting their left arm around their partner. All dance forward and the "star" rotates once around. All then turn individually and reform a "star," men now joining left hands, right arms around partners, to return to place. In Conception Harbour, left hands are joined first. In both Conception Harbour and Pouch Cove, this followed and was considered a figure in the same part of the dance as the "basket." All three "baskets" are formed by the men crossing arms and linking hands with the man next to them.

The women link their arms with the men's elbows, forming a tightly knit circle, which then rotates twice in each direction. In Trinity, the linked arms are raised and lowered in the center with increasing energy through one strain of the tune. I was told that it was usual to lift the women off the floor during the last spin of the circle.

The "longways reel" figure is performed in lines, or longways formation, which would be assumed during a break in the music. Partners face each other, the head couples at top and bottom of the set, side couples in between. The top couple begins by swinging together and then progressing down the set, alternately swinging their partner and each person of the opposite sex in turn. In Trinity, this was done by turning once around by the left hand on the sides, and once by the right hand with partners in the center. The other two versions describe the movement as a closed position swing. In the Trinity performance, once each couple reached the bottom of the set they side-stepped to the top and back again to the bottom between the two lines. All then faced down the set and took four side steps to their right, and then back to their left. The lines passed through one another, the women in front of their partners. The lines then "cast off" from the bottom, marching up the outside of the set individually, down again through the top and back to place. From this position, the next couple began the "longways reel" and the entire sequence was repeated for each couple.

The final group figures of the Lancers, "right and left" and "thread the needle," are also found in some versions of the Square Dance, with some variation. In Trinity, dancers face their partners and bow to begin the chain, go halfway around the set, where they meet their partners for the first time, bow again and swing. They continue to chain, bowing and swinging with each one they meet until original partners are reunited in place. In Pouch Cove, where the figure is left (hand to partners) and right (hand to the next) after one circuit of chaining, the men and women similarly swing their partners, chain once around again then swing the next, and so forth. In Conception Harbour, after the first circuit of chaining, partners swing and then reverse direction, chaining back the other way.

"Thread the needle" is performed as a final figure in Pouch Cove and Conception Harbour; in the former community it is known as "spin the needle." It is the same figure as that found in the Square Dance. The similar structure of the different square dances made adaptation and borrowing from one to another quite simple. I have already noted that the "thread the needle" figure was considered optional in the Square Dance. It could just as easily be added to the Lancers if, as a man from Conception Harbour describes it in the following story, the dancers hadn't "had enough" after the "longways reel":

> We just finished playin' the Lancers an' Master Keating didn't have enough. He called for more music an' we had to play ya know, coz them times people got real mad if ya didn't do what dey said. Well, we started 'er up again an' Jack got his crew on d' floor an started t' tread d' needle set. Dis was d' first time 'twas ever done. It don't belong t'd Lancers. Na! It's part o'd' American Eight. An dat's how d' Lancers got t' be five sets now instid o' four.[59]

The presence of the "thread the needle" in other variants belies the specific aetiological claim of this explanatory tale. Rather, it relates a scenario undoubtedly enacted many times when the Lancers became popular.

The Lancers, like the Square Dance, begins with crossing movements and concludes with join together and exchange partner figures. Its three central distinctive figures distinguish it most clearly from the Square Dance. There is some variation of the "star," "basket," and "longways reel" figures. Structurally, the two are much the same. The smaller, four couple Lancers' set, however, allows more integration of the end and side couples throughout the dance in the form of more frequent alternations and "corner swings".

Another difference between the dances is expressed in informants' attitudes towards them. In Trinity, where both dances were known and performed at the same events, the Square Dance was considered rougher than the more sedate and sophisticated Lancers. Music for the Square Dance was provided by the accordion, while for the Lancers the local, female, school teacher and a friend played the violin and piano. Only a few dancers were considered to know the Lancers well enough to perform it, while everyone could get through the Square Dance.[60] Vestiges of ballroom etiquette, such as the bow after exchanging partners in part two or upon meeting in the "right and left," reflect these attitudes in movement. In other reports where the Lancers is the only group dance mentioned, no such distinctions are made.

It appears that these dances are nearly identical in structure and owe their differences to the historical sources from which they come. The Lancers was one of the most popular late 19th century quadrilles. It was introduced in England in 1817, revived in the 1850s and by the end of the century had developed many local variations in common performance, which were dubbed the Kitchen Lancers by dancing teachers of the time.[61] The Newfoundland versions are probably derived from these folk versions or were introduced through the late-19th century revival.

The Reel

Another group dance in square formation reported in Newfoundland is frequently called the Reel. Although its basic movements and minor units are similar to those of the Square Dance and Lancers, the organization of figures is different. The two couple figures are not performed by alternating groups of facing couples, but rather progressively, each couple in the set dancing in turn with all the others. In the usual four couple set, numbering the couples around it counter-clockwise, the first would dance a figure in turn with the second, third, and fourth couples. Each couple then repeats this pattern in turn.

I was never able to get a good description of the Reel while in Plate Cove, but it was frequently mentioned. Mick Keough, for instance, recalled,

> That'd be eight hands out [i.e., the Reel], four men and four girls. That's a long dance too . . . I used to play for them here years ago.[62]

Fortunately however, the English folksong and dance collector, Maud Karpeles, while visiting nearby Stock Cove in 1929, saw the Reel (along with the Square and Kissing Dances) performed and described it in her notes as follows:

THE REEL

Performed by 6 couples when I saw it, but it can be and is, I think, usually performed by 4 couples.

As in Running Set, each couple leads out the figure in turn, but numbering round counter-clockwise.

The step is very much the same as in the Sets, something between a walk and a run.

Each of the four figures starts with the following introduction.

Introduction

Hands all to center and back twice.

Men step (8 bars).

Swing partners (8 bars).

Grand Chain, giving hands, or sometimes arms (but not turning).

Swing partners.

The following movements are interpolated between the leads of the successive couples.

Swing partners, Grand Chain. Swing partners. Grand Chain is called 'Bush'.

1st Figure

1st couple takes hands with the 2nd couple, step, and then hands-four, and so on to each couple in turn.

2nd Figure

1st man arms partner with right, 2nd man left, partner right and so on.

Each man performs this figure in turn and then the women.

3rd Figure

1st couple lead forward and back.

Lead through 2nd couple and cast off round outside of set to places, and so on to next couple.

4th Figure

All take hands, except 1st man and 2nd woman.

1st man, followed by others, leads under arch made by 1st woman and her contrary partner, and so on passing under successive arches (as in Grape Vine Swing) except that all dancers are moving round clockwise all the time.

This is called "Thread the needle."[63]

There are few other descriptions of the Reel to be found among my sources; however, the Goat, a dance referred to as a "cotillion" and collected in Harbour Deep, is similarly structured.[64] It includes the same figures, as well as a few additional patterns.

Although the organization of the Reel is somewhat different from the Square Dance and Lancers, the structural system is closely related. All three prescribe floor designs and dancer direction, using individual, partner, two couple, and whole group interactions. Despite their symmetrical, repetitive form, each contains a progressive sequence of distinctive figures, beginning with two couple interactions and culminating in whole group patterns. In the Reel however, the join together and exchange partner movements are incorporated throughout the dance, rather than only in the final section.

Longways Dances

Though performed from a different formation, the longways dances have many of the same structural features as the square and other group dances. The division of dancers into male and female roles is still fundamental. In this case, although partnered they are also grouped by sex from the beginning. The basic movements are similar: dancers move around and across the set, they interact as individuals, partners, couples, and groups of men or women. The dances are similar in construction and are not divided into parts as the Square Dance or Lancers. Like the Reel, they repeat their figures progressively for each couple in turn. I have no information on the usual size of these sets, but suspect they varied considerably.

Longways dances are much less frequently reported than the mostly quadrille-derived square dances. Maud Karpeles published notations for two, which were described to her by Dick Penny of Burin, a musician who played the flute and violin.[65] One of these, the Self, has a distinctive circling figure while the other, Kitty's Rambles, employs a "hey," or a weaving figure. Each dance also employs traveling through the set and swinging as secondary figures.

Sir Roger was described to me as a dance typically performed on Random Island. Its figures are derived from Sir Roger de Coverly, a dance found in Playford's *Dancing Master* of 1696 which since then has undergone periodic revival, as Chappell commented in 1859.[66] This same dance is likewise the basis for the Virginia Reel, popular throughout North America and reported in Plate Cove as well.[67]

Sir Roger was performed in longways formation and the figures were described as follows:

> Top couple dance down the center and back, apparently backing up, in open position, twice. They cast off, down the outside and the other dancers follow. The top couple forms an arch and the others go under it, returning to their original place. The top man and his "opposite partner" (i.e., the bottom woman) [the first corners] turn by the right elbow. The top woman and bottom man do likewise [the second corners]. The first corners and then the second, turn left elbow, then go back to back passing left, and then right shoulders. The top couple perform a Longway's reel to the bottom and all swing their partners. The dance then repeats with a new top couple.[68]

The longways dances are, as Karpeles observed, much like the English country dances revived by Cecil Sharp and the English Country Dance and Song Society. They would have been part of the repertoire brought by immigrants from Britain and were probably replaced by the quadrille-derived dances, much as they were in England, during the latter nineteenth century.

The Kissing Dance

The Kissing Dance is another group dance, but quite different from the square and longways dances already discussed. It has changed significantly within my informants' recollection and I will take up the different versions in turn. All begin with an incremental sequence in which dancers join the performance one at a time. This process culminates in a join together movement.

Two variants of this dance were recorded and published by Maud Karpeles. The first was demonstrated to her in the lobby of the Newfoundland Hotel by Mr. P.K. Devine, a local historian and folksong enthusiast, who was also harbour master in St. John's, and a native of King's Cove.[69] She noted at the time:

> After lunch, Mr. Devine called to see me. An interesting old man and a great talker. I took down the tune of Cushion Dance from him much to amusement of bell boys as he tramped round whilst singing it, finally kneeling down in front of me and presenting me with the cushion (i.e. my newspaper).[70]

A few days later, when she saw the dance performed in Stock Cove, it was accompanied by an accordion player without the dancers singing. One man held a handkerchief in front of him and danced around the room. He chose one of the women, whom he kissed, behind (or sometimes through) the handkerchief. She then took it and stood in front of him. He placed his hands on her shoulders and they danced around until she similarly chose a man. According to Karpeles, this continued until all were chosen. The dancers then formed a ring around the last one chosen, who sat in the center. This person then chose someone from the ring, kissed them and gave them the handkerchief. They then sat, chose another from the ring, and so on until all were again chosen.[71]

The import of this pantomime was not lost on Miss Karpeles who writes in her notes as follows:

> Confess I felt a little embarrassed at joining in the dance because I knew that being the guest of honor I would be the first chosen by the very handsome young man who was standing in the center. However, all was well because I found that the handkerchief, instead of being placed on the floor and knelt on, was discreetly placed between our faces when the kiss took place.

In contemporary performances, which I have seen, the handkerchief has been used, playfully, as a screen behind which the dancers kiss.

My Plate Cove informants recalled the dance similarly, though they placed less emphasis on the first part. Mick

Keough described it as follows:

> The Kissing Dance? Yes, used to have that . . . all the girls and fellas would line up, see, in a ring. And a fella put a chair in the center, sat down in the center. And he had a handkerchief see. And he had it up this way (holds it in front of his face). There's a tune for it we used to call "the Fool." We'd put a bit of rhyme on it, "Now you fool you're in the ring, you won't get out till the eighth of spring" (laughter). . . . Then he'd kiss someone then. He'd kiss a girl and the girl would sit down, see. Somebody'd be playing, see, the tune. . . [then] she'd kiss a fella and he'd have to sit down. Till everyone, perhaps there'd be maybe thirty or forty, fellas and girls. Now the last fella he was, he had no one to kiss out, see (laugh), he was the fool in the ring.

He recalled concluding this sequence with the opening movements of "off she goes" from the Square Dance. The dancers also, apparently, performed a "flirtation" after this, which was similar to the final "ladies in" of the Square Dance.

> Flirtation they used to have it, see. Ladies would get on the floor and if they want to have a step they'd have it. They set back then . . . to their partners. They'd have a "left and right." Go around . . . one would come up on this side and the other and you go right around the whole ring, till you come to your partner again.[73]

Mick's daughter recalled the chair sequence as well, but with a different rhyme again. As she described it, when there was no one left to kiss for the last one in the chair,

> then they'll at him and say, "Now old man you're down for this." . . . He's in the ring sitting on this chair like a fool, eh, and they going around.[74]

According to Therese, however, and as taught by the Red Cliff Dancers, in more recent years the second, subtractive sequence was usually eliminated, and once the ring of dancers had been formed, the concluding join together figures were performed. Structurally, then, the Kissing Dance as performed in the Plate Cove region has been adapted to the same form as the other group dances; progressing from partner interactions to couple and group patterns.

Maud Karpeles noted the similarity of this dance to the historical Cushion Dance, traced by Chappell to an obscure reference in 1580. He gives the earliest full description of this dance from the 1686 edition of Playford's *Dancing Master*.[75] In *The Traditional Games of England, Scotland and Ireland,* Gomme cites numerous examples collected in England.[76] In all these historical versions dancers kneel on a cushion rather than holding up a handkerchief. Karpeles was told in Stock Cove that

> originally dancers used to carry a cushion on which the lady knelt before her choice, but that a handkerchief had been substituted for a cushion and gradually the kneeling had dropped out, so that the handkerchief had lost its original use.[77]

The Kissing Dance, while probably derived from the Cushion Dance, is also related to the games often substituted for dances because of religious principles. Frequently called ring games in Newfoundland, these are also commonly referred to as singing games in most of the folklore literature about them. Gomme's versions of the Cushion Dance suggest this relationship as well, illustrating, in her words, a "transition from a dance to a pure game."[78]

In her study of Indiana games, Leah Wolford has grouped together those "in which choosing is the most important feature." She observes of them:

> Thirty years ago practically every choosing game was a "kissing game" . . . . Today, the "kissing games" are either not played or have been changed so as to omit this characteristic feature. In place of choosing partners has come, it seems, a further development of the dance.[79]

A similar evolution from partner choosing game to dance is apparent among versions of the Newfoundland Kissing Dance.

The extent of crossover between dance and game forms is probably quite large. Aubrey Tizzard, for example, recalled such dance games as Tucker, Sir Roger, and the Ring, along with Musical Chairs, and Spin the Bottle, as typical of dance events in his Notre Dame Bay community.[80] What distinguished some of these games from dances is not always clear. I have already discussed Sir Roger as a dance and, according to Mr. Tizzard, Tucker "was sort of a dance performance, yet not a dance."[81] The boundaries are blurred further by the use of instrumental music, in this case an accordion, and not just singing to accompany the games. Vocal imitations of instrumental music and snatches of sung verse were often used to accompany dances as well.

In general, games place more emphasis on dramatic devices than dances. Dance movement seems more stylized and abstract than the pantomimic game actions. There are, however, many continuities between game and dance movement forms. While participants found it convenient to so distinguish them, the form and functions of games are so nearly identical to those of dance behavior that further study is needed to elaborate on their relationship.[82] In this work, I have confined myself generally to those expressions identified by informants as dance.

Summary

There are many dances performed traditionally in Newfoundland which I have not described in this chapter, nor have all available variants of those I have described been noted in complete detail. Rather than the compilation of such a catalogue, perhaps useful in its own right, my purpose has been to illustrate the major forms of Newfoundland folk dance and analyze their choreographic structure.

Underlying all the dance movement I have described is a characteristic use of the body, which calls for an upright posture, single unit torso, and maintenance of the body axis. Movement is articulated below the waist and the feet generally remain directly under the body. Dances are organized as group, individual, and couple forms, the first two types predominating.

The group dances are highly articulated in floor plan and distinguished one from another on this basis. They may consist of one distinctive figure, as do the longways dances, combined with a standard repertoire of secondary figures, or several distinctive figures may be done in sequence, along with secondary movements, as parts of a longer dance. The latter form, usually in square formation, seems to predominate. Partner, couple, and group movements may be mixed together, as in the Reel, or performed in a progressive sequence, as in the Square Dance, Lancers, and Kissing Dance.

As an individual form, step dancing is largely improvisational, although there are a few widely known traditional steps. Performances are constructed by combining short step sequences together. While an ideal structural form may be acknowledged, in practice the improvisatory character of the dance dominates. Dancers do, however, make an effort to increase the complexity and excitement of their movements as the performance progresses. To do this they employ both the sound of their stepping and the visual impact of their movements.

Variation of the group dances is found within certain acknowledged traditional norms. Among different performances of the same dance, even within one region or by the same dancers, variation is possible through changes in the duration of minor movement units or substitutions of equivalent movements, such as a step dance sequence for a partners spin. Regional variation among versions of the same dance is found in the different characteristic secondary figures employed to elaborate the prescribed distinctive figures. Throughout Newfoundland, however, the distinctive figures and structural framework of each dance remain relatively constant in all versions.

NOTES — CHAPTER 2

1. *Public Ledger,* 29 May 1857, p. 2 , col. 4.

2. *Evening Telegram,* 11 Dec. 1879, p.1, col. 2.

3. See Joann Kealiinohomoku, "Folk Dance," in *Folklore and Folklife: An Introduction,* ed. Richard Dorson (Chicago: University of Chicago Press, 1972), pp. 382-404, for a definition and discussion of this term.

4. Ruth Katz, "The Egalitarian Waltz," *Comparative Studies in Society and History,* 15 (1973), 368-97.

5. Throughout this study, I have capitalized such terms as *Square Dance* when used as the title of a particular dance. As a generic term it appears in lower case. Conventional titles for its parts are set in lower case in quotation marks.

6. MUNFLA, Ms., 81-271/p. 23; Tape, 81-271/C5186.

7. I have discussed these distinctions in more detail in "Singles, Doubles, and Triples: Musical Terminology in Placentia Bay," Folklore Studies Association of Canada Meeting, Montreal, 1980. The sources for this paper were MUNFLA, MS., 81-271/pp. 437-39; and MUNFLA, Tape, 79-54/C4107, 4108.

8. MUNFLA, Ms., 81-271/p. 39.

9. MUNFLA, Ms., 81-271/p. 126. The tempo of playing is in fact faster than that of the Harbour Buffett examples.

10. MUNFLA, Ms., 75-25/p. 14.

11. A good discussion of this observation may be found in Ljubica S. Janković. "Paradoxes in the Living Creative Process of Dance Tradition," *Ethnomusicology,* 13 (1969), 124-28.

12. See "Good Entertainment '77, Part B," (Memorial University of Newfoundland Educational T.V., cat. # 10 304, 1979), for a videotape recording of such a performance.

13. MUNFLA, Ms., 81-271/pp. 177-81. Gerald Quinton expressed these opinions, which I found were shared by most informants.

14. MUNFLA, Ms., 73-174/p. 21; Ms., 73-89/p. 8; MS., 81-271/pp. 198, 273.

15. Personal Communication from Herbert Halpert, May 1981.

16. *Dictionary of Newfoundland English,* eds. G.M.Story, W.J.Kirwin, J.D.A.Widdowson (Toronto: University of Toronto Press, 1982), p. 571.

17. MUNFLA, Ms., 79-339/p. 24.

18. MUNFLA, Ms., 81-271/p. 198.

19. Personal communication from Herbert Halpert, May 1981. See Colin Quigley, "Folk Dance and Dance Events in Rural Newfoundland," M.A. Thesis, Memorial University of Newfoundland, 1981.

20. See Richard Nevell, *A Time to Dance* (New York: St. Martin's Press, 1977), p. 48; and Chris Brady, "Appalachian Clogging," *English Dance and Song*, 43:1 (1981), 12-13, for photographic examples of this style.

21. MUNFLA, Ms., 79-339/p. 55.

22. MUNFLA, Ms., 81-271/p. 147.

23. This may be clearly seen during the dance shown in *Introduction to Fogo Island*, National Film Board of Canada # 106B 0168 065, n.d. The men step dance vigorously while holding their practically motionless partners in a closed social dance position.

24. MUNFLA, Ms., 73-89/p. 109.

25. MUNFLA, Ms., 77-334/p. 20B.

26. MUNFLA, Ms., 73-174/p. 19.

27. MUNFLA, Ms., 73-174/p. 21, is one instance.

28. Brendán Breathnach, *Folkmusic and Dances of Ireland* (Dublin: Talbot Press, 1971), p. 48.

29. J.G. O'Keefe and Art O'Brien, *A Handbook of Irish Dances: With an Essay on their Origin and History* (Dublin: M.H. Gill, 1954), p. 107.

30. Breathnach, pp. 63-64.

31. MUNFLA, Ms., 73-174/p. 19; a similar teaching jingle from Ireland may be found in Breathnach, p. 56.

32. MUNFLA, Ms., 81-271/p. 439.

33. MUNFLA, Ms., 81-271/p. 438.

34. "Good Entertainment '77, Part B."

35. MUNFLA. Ms., 75-25/p. 14.

36. MUNFLA. Ms., 77-334/p. 19; Ms., 73-174/p. 20; Ms., 75-25/p. 14.

37. Gerald's discussion of his step dancing is in my field notes, MUNFLA, Ms., 81-271/p. 177. For a notation of these steps see my M.A. Thesis, pp. 224-27.

38. MUNFLA, Ms., 77-339/p. 58.

39. J.F. and T.M. Flett, *Traditional Step-Dancing in Lakeland* (London: English Folk Dance and Song Society, 1979), pp. vi-vii.

40. MUNFLA, Ms., 79-339/p. 43.

41. Cecil Sharp and A.P. Oppé, *The Dance* (London: Halton and Truscott Smith; New York: Minton, Balch & Co., 1924), pp. 12-13.

42. Joseph Strutt, *The Sports and Pastimes of the People of England* (1801, 1903; rpt. Bath: Firecrest, 1969), p. 177.

43. Breathnach p. 45.

44. MUNFLA, Ms., 72-124/p. 14. This phrase is reported from Ireland as well in O'Keefe, p. 110; and, Capt. Francis O'Neill, *Irish Folk Music: A Fascinating Hobby* (1910; rpt. Darby, PA: Norwood Editions, 1973), pp. 300-01.

45. Some interesting examples of these are cited together with a discussion of the Double in MUNFLA, Ms., 77-334/pp. 21-23. They include such physical feats as standing on one's head or balancing on a small object.

46. Len Margaret (Mary Pittman), *Fish & Brewis, Toutens and Tales: Recipes and Recollections from St. Leonard's, Newfoundland,* Canada's Atlantic Folklore and Folklife Series, No. 7 (St. John's: Breakwater, 1980), p. 8.

47. MUNFLA, Ms., 81-271/p. 286.

48. MUNFLA, Ms., 81-271/p. 302.

49. Personal communication from Anne McLeod concerning the dancers she filmed in Harbour Deep, MUNFLA, Ms., 81-271 /p. 443.

50. MUNFLA, Ms., 81-271/p. 147.

51. Burt Feintuch, "Dancing to the Music: Domestic Square Dances and Community in South Central Kentucky (1880-1940)," *Journal of the Folklore Institute,* 18 (1981), 49-69.

52. MUNFLA, Videotape, 78-364/v. 39, 42. For a notation based on this performance see my M.A. thesis, pp. 96-152.

53. This term is commonly used in discussions of dance forms with a repertoire of basic floor patterns that are used in many dances.

54. MUNFLA, Ms., 81-271/p. 179.

55. Philip Richardson, *The Social Dances of the Nineteenth Century in England* (London: Herbert Jenkins, 1960), pp. 134-41.

56. Richardson, p. 138.

57. Descriptions of the dances compared are from the following sources: Red Cliff, MUNFLA, Ms., 78-364/v. 39, 42; Stock Cove, MUNFLA, Ms., 78-003/folder 2, pp. 4690-93; New Perlican, MUNFLA, Ms., 79-630; Trouty, MUNFLA, Ms., 73-147; Port de Grave, MUNFLA, Ms., 73-89; Tack's Beach, Jacquey Ryan, "Dancing in Tack's Beach with Mrs. E. Best," unpublished Ms., 1980, in the author's collection; Bay d'Espoir, MUNFLA, Ms., 71-146; Forteau, my field work, MUNFLA, Ms., 81-271/pp. 276-85.

58. These dances are described in the following sources: MUNFLA, Ms., 81-271/pp. 360-66, 429-35; Ms., 80-118/9-22.

59. MUNFLA, Ms., 80-118/p. 35.

60. MUNFLA, Ms., 81-271/p. 358.

61. See Richardson, pp. 70-73, 91-94; and Roy Dommett, "The Kitchen Lancers," *English Dance and Song,* 4:3 (1979), 7.

62. MUNFLA, Ms., 81-271/p. 100.

63. MUNFLA, Ms., 78-003/folder 2, pp. 4694-95.

64. MUNFLA, Ms., 72-155; MUNFLA, Videotape, 80-126; ''A Square Dance,'' Memorial University Extension Media Service, 1979.

65. Maud Karpeles, *Twelve Traditional Dances* (London: Novello, 1931), pp. 16-17.

66. William Chappell, *Popular Music of the Olden Time* (1859; rpt. New York: Dover, 1965), II, 531-35.

67. MUNFLA, Ms., 81-271/p. 68.

68. MUNFLA, Ms., 81-271/pp. 380-81.

69. Maud Karpeles, *Folk Songs of Newfoundland* (London: Faber and Faber, 1971), p. 256.

70. MUNFLA, Ms., 78-003/folder 1, 11 Sept. 1929.

71. These descriptions are taken from Karpeles, *Folk Songs*, pp. 256-57.

72. MUNFLA, Ms., 78-003/folder 8, pp. 23-24.

73. Mick's descriptions are in MUNFLA, Ms., 81-271/pp. 101-03.

74. MUNFLA, Ms., 81-271/p. 108.

75. Chappell, I, 153-57.

76. Alice Bertha Gomme, *The Traditional Games of England, Scotland and Ireland* (1894; rpt. New York: Dover, 1964), I, 87-94.

77. MUNFLA, Ms., 78-003/folder 2, pp. 4696-97.

78. Gomme, I, 92-93.

79. Leah Wolford, *The Play Party in Indiana*, Indiana Historical Society Publications, Vol. 20, No. 2, ed. W. Edson Richmond and William Tillson (Indianapolis: Indianapolis Historical Society, 1959), pp. 127-28.

80. Aubrey Tizzard, *On Sloping Ground: Reminiscences of Outport Life in Notre Dame Bay, Newfoundland*, Memorial University Folklore and Language Publications, Community Studies Series No. 2, ed. J.D.A. Widdowson (St. John's: Memorial University of Newfoundland, 1979), pp. 228-29.

81. Tizzard, p. 230.

82. B.A. Botkin, *The American Play-Party Song* (1937; rpt. New York: Frederick Ungar, 1963), pp. 37-53.

CHAPTER 3: The Dances in Context

While traditional dance in Newfoundland has historical antecedents and shares many common characteristics with British/North American traditions generally, it has also been molded by its local context. Dances, as events, ritualized and set apart from everyday activities, are occasions in which social norms and cultural values are often strongly exemplified.[1] They are a form of structured nonverbal communication among the dancers and onlookers.[2] Their movements facilitate the pursuit of the dancers' individual goals and so embody the social functions which animate the dance events. They are enactments of the social relations among the participants. The special qualities of vernacular dancing in Newfoundland may be found in the adaptation of traditional forms to the expressive needs of the dancers and other dance event participants. Analysis of the dance movements must view them as one aspect of the dance event contexts, which, with associated behaviors and conceptions, make up the society's dance culture.[3] I will, therefore, consider in turn: the situations in which dancers use different movements; what the dancers say about their movements; and the relationship of dance to everyday conventions of nonverbal communication.[4]

Occasions for dancing

There are a number of occasions at which dancing may be expected and people used a large number of terms when identifying them. The significance of these terms for analysis is twofold. First, they label categories and distinctions recognized within the dance culture. The word "time," for example, is applied to many dance events, as it refers not to a specific social event, but rather to any party, especially one with singing and dancing.[5] Times, furthermore, are occasions characterized by sanctioned deviation from the norms of social behavior. Drinking and sexual joking of a manner normally thought out of order are indulged in and expected.[6] Most dance events could be described as times. Second, the terminology indicates some aspects of the events on which distinctions are based. These include: where and when it was held, as for example a "kitchen racket," "stove time," "bridge dance," or "Christmas spree"; who participated, as, for example, a "joined ball" to which one had to subscribe; or what other activities might or might not be expected to take place, as at a "garden party" run by the local parish, or a "hungry dance" at which no food was to be served. There is some overlap among these terms. Thus the dancing at a garden party could be described as a "hall time," while a dance on Candlemas could be a kitchen racket. Although each dance event is a unique occurrence there are patterns to which they conform and by these designations people identify a particular configuration of variables. Dance events may occur on fixed calendar celebrations, at certain seasons of the year, in response to occupationally related events, such as the return of men from the Labrador fishery, or at more spontaneous social gatherings; they take place out-of-doors, in public buildings, or private homes; and they may include participants from several nearby communities, one community or "place," a social organization, "crowd,"[7] or age group. Despite this variety some general distinctions may be made.

Many dance events were community festivals recalled as high points of the social year. Most communities had at least one and often several such events during the year, usually held during the Christmas season or on other calendar or seasonal occasions. Dancing was almost always the culmination of these festivals. The dancing was often formally organized with recognized social roles assigned to particular individuals. One "fiddler," that is, an accordion or violin player, was hired to play for the entire dance. A floor manager, or master, was often appointed to keep order. The group figure dances were typical of these events, interspersed with a few individual step dances and sometimes a Waltz.

Another class of dance events, attended by smaller groups of people, were usually less formally organized and more spontaneous. They might occur whenever enough people felt like dancing, but were most common during the winter season. Many musicians might play for the dancing and the mouth organ, jews harp, and "chin music" (i.e., vocal accompaniment) were commonly used, as well as the accordion or violin. Similar dances were performed as at the larger festivals, but in smaller sets, and with less formal organization. Other performance genres, such as singing and storytelling, were also much more prominent at these events.

Informants often distinguished these two major categories of Newfoundland dance events as "hall" and "house" times. Their contextual characteristics are summarized below in Table 3.

TABLE 3

CONTEXTUAL COMPARISON OF TIMES

	Hall Times	House Times
Where	public building	private building
When	calendar or seasonal	seasonal or spontaneous
Who	regional, community, or formal institution	kinship, work, or age group "crowd"

The distinction between these events is clearly reflected by people's attitudes towards them. At the house times "you could let your hair down," while behavior at the hall times, subject to a more public scrutiny, was therefore more circumspect.[8] Although other combinations among the contextual factors are possible, most dance events may be ranged along this spectrum of formality. These general distinctions are significant, but in order to understand the social dynamics which create them, we must turn to more detailed descriptions of the dance events.

Hall Times

Hall times were often organized by the church or other formal institutions and used by them to raise money. They include garden parties, Christmas sprees, and times sponsored by fraternal organizations. Along with dancing, food preparation and consumption became a formally organized social expression. Social drinking of beer and liquor was typical among the men, but remained informal and was not often allowed in the hall itself. Specific occasions might include other practices such as gift exchange at Christmas, a parade by lodge members at the Orangemen's time, or games of chance at the garden parties and other fund-raising affairs.

Garden Parties

Throughout Newfoundland generally the term ''garden party'' refers to a summer gathering usually held on the grounds of the local church, where games and contests are held, food served, and funds raised for the parish. They are similar to church fund-raisings elsewhere in North America.[9]

George Casey has described the garden party as the biggest social event of the year in Conche, a community on the Northern Peninsula. Although a means to help finance the building and maintenance of schools and churches it also provided a welcome break in summer work. This celebration provided opportunities for young people to meet prospective mates and the adults expected every young man to have a ''date'' for the occasion. If one did not he often became the butt of jokes concerning his failure ''to get a girl and there were lots of 'em here.'' Casey further notes that the opportunity to work together for the good of the church and the image of the community tended to build community solidarity.[10]

Until the 1970s the Garden Party appears to have been one of the major occasions for dancing in the Plate Cove region. Each community, or ''every place around,'' would have a garden party during the summer which attracted people from all the nearby communities. People came to Plate Cove from Sweet Bay, Summerville, Open Hall, Red Cliff, Tickle Cove, King's Cove, Duntara and Knight's Cove. These garden parties featured games of chance in the afternoon, a supper in the evening and a dance at night. The entire event required a high degree of social organization to produce, and preparations were often co-ordinated by the schoolmaster.

In Conche preparations were made through the election

of a men's and women's committee. The men were responsible for providing for the physical necessities, such as tables
and chairs, building booths, and installing extra stoves. The
women were responsible for deciding the menu of the supper to be served, its preparation, selling tickets, and attending to the various booths.[11] In Plate Cove there was a
similar formalization of preparations.

The garden party dance was also formally organized. It
was usually held in the school or parish hall after the supper
was cleared away. In Plate Cove a single musician was hired,
almost always an accordion player. Although someone might
take his place to allow him a rest, this musician would, in
fact, play throughout the night. A floor manager was
sometimes appointed to keep order and ensure that everyone
had an opportunity to dance.

Mrs. Keough recalled the garden parties in this way:

> Well I'll tell you what it was like one time. What you do
> is pay a dollar, a dollar fifty as you be going, what the old
> peoples call "on the door." Well, a fine day, fine after-
> noon, the desk would be out by the entrance coming in
> on the grounds and they would, uh, collect the money
> there and give you a ticket. And that entitles you then to
> your supper.
>
> . . . .
>
> Oh yes, out under the grounds, there would be probably
> Bingo, and would be swings for the children. And there
> would be all kinds of games and everything. And then they
> would have the gun, what they used to call the gun,
> shooting at the bull's eye, eh. . . . See who, you know,
> who'd go close to the bull's eye. And, oh yeah, made quite
> a lot of money then. Because I mean everybody would
> donate things, eh.[12]

In some communities, dancing took place out of doors
during the daylight hours as another fund-raising activity.
At one garden party in Placentia, for example, a dancing platform was erected where one could dance to an accordion
player's music for 5 cents a dance.[13]

Supper followed the afternoon fund-raising activities, and
was served in the school building. In the meantime many
of the men had been visiting around the community drink-

ing in each house, or perhaps in their cars. Eventually, perhaps by 11:00 p.m., the tables were cleared away and the dance could begin.[14]

Mrs. Geraldine Keough remembered the crowded square dances with "twenty-five or thirty dancers" on the floor at once, indicating the largest sets possible.[15] If a figure like "change partners" was done, "where all the girls had to swing with every fella was on the floor," it might take as long as an hour to get through the dance. Throughout the night there would be only six or seven such dances. She recalled at one time the musician was paid by collection:

> First that I can remember, used to go around with the hat and take up a collection. . . . But that was more or less in my mother's time, 'cause we weren't allowed to stay there that late in the night. . . . We would just be allowed to stay and watch one or two dances, 'till nine-thirty or ten o'clock. We'd have to go home then. I can see 'em going out, someone taking up, with a hat, taking up a collection.[16]

In later years this became a formal fee, although it was always minimal. Mrs. Patricia Keough recalled that in more recent years this might be as much as twenty-five or thirty dollars, although her father often played all night for only two dollars.[17] Larry Barker, for many years the musician hired for garden parties throughout the region, considered his services a donation to the church.[18]

Several informants commented on the practice of holding a smaller, "community-only," dance a short time after the garden party. In Long Harbour, Placentia Bay, for instance, the garden party was not considered ended until the Friday night following the weekend celebration. A big closing dance would be held on that night, which many found more enjoyable "because there were fewer people around."[19] In Fermeuse, the Garden Party dance was always held on a Sunday night, but the following Tuesday another, usually better, dance was held without any "outsiders."[20]

Such comments call attention to the regional, intercommunity nature of the garden party gatherings. For the successful performance of the group dances the participants depend upon a shared knowledge of the dance. The maxim which I heard repeatedly that "each place does the dance a bit differently" is an important one which reflects the importance attached to this social unit. Naturally, the smaller, locally residential group would perform the dances more satisfyingly than the large group attending the garden party from outlying areas. More subtlety and variety was possible within the smaller group. The regional group required more formal structuring of the event in order to accommodate large numbers of dancers, but at any size the dancing seems to give expression to the shared membership of the participants in a single social group.

However, reports of overt conflict at these events are also frequent. Mrs. Geraldine Keough recalled:

> Used to be a scattered fight years ago but I don't remember that much. I often heard my grandmother saying there's a garden party over there between here and John Dooley's [a nearby house] . . . . Their names were Cheevers, and they had a garden party over there. I used to hear tell of it. . . . It could be back in the twenties. And it was only open two hours and they made five hundred dollars. But they had to close it because the big racket started. And that was as good as a million dollars now, or half a million anyway, five hundred dollars, them times. Anyhow, they made five hundred dollars and it was open two hours and they had to close it down because the big racket started (laughter).[21]

According to Gerald Quinton, there were so many dancers fighting to get onto the floor at the garden parties that the floor master was needed to keep order. He explained:

> There was lots of moonshine "on the go" then and the men would have a few drinks and get to feeling pretty good. It wouldn't take much then to start a fight.[22]

Others likewise commented that the moonshine drunk outside the school by the men often contributed to the eruption of fights at the dances. Drinking also took place on the community wharf, but fights were apparently less common here. While the occasional fight was tolerated any property damage was not, and the culprits, if caught, were expected to stay away from future community times.[23]

Expressions of conflict which had developed between individuals in every day interaction were apparently common at these dances. Inhibitions were broken down by alcohol consumption, and conflicts appear to have been aggravated by the large size and multi-community nature of the gatherings. I suspect that the social sanctions against the violent expression of conflict which normally function in the small, closely knit outport societies did not work as strongly in these larger, more anonymous groups. The informal restrictions had then to be supplemented by formal regulations such as no alcohol in the hall, and the appointment of a floor manager to keep order. From the available descriptions it is difficult to know whether these conflicts erupted between members of the same or different places. The mention of such distinctions by informants, however, suggests that lack of restraints affecting members of different communities may also contribute to the high level of conflict expressed.

Usually, though, the celebratory, festive nature of these gatherings is emphasized. George Casey describes this ideal character of the event as follows:

> Although there was lots of drinking throughout the period of the garden party, the whole atmosphere was one of congeniality and rarely did any conflicts develop. Hospitality, generosity and friendliness were evident everywhere. Behaviour was certainly different at the garden party, as it was at any of "the times" or community social events, than it was in usual daily interaction. Behaviour and comments normally thought to be improper, especially in mixed company, were now excused, and people danced, sang and told jokes and stories that were mildly bawdy.[24]

The idealized conception of this event emphasizes sexuality, courtship and communal concord. Expressions of concomitant rivalries and ongoing conflicts are downplayed and considered as intrusive elements not really a part of the garden party event.

Christmas Sprees

In Tickle Cove, a community only a few miles down the bay from Plate Cove, the church-sponsored times were called "sprees" and were held once during the Christmas season. In the first decades of this century sprees were held to raise money for the upkeep of church and school buildings. Like the garden parties, they were patronized by the surrounding communities. They were structured similarly to the garden party, but conditioned by different environmental specifics, such as the season, geography, and community religious affiliation.

As reported by a student collector whose work I have paraphrased, and quoted from below, due to the religious affiliations of local communities, Tickle Cove sprees were held on a weeknight during the Christmas season.[25] The Roman Catholic parish church was three miles away in Open Hall and Mass was held early in the morning, which made it inconvenient for Tickle Cove Catholics to hold a dance on Saturday night. No fund-raising supper could be held on Friday because the Catholics could not eat meat, and the largely Protestant residents of Red Cliff would not attend a dance on Sunday. The weeknight date was set perhaps a week or two in advance to avoid clashing with events in other communities and give the priest an opportunity to announce the event at services throughout the parish and make an appeal for generosity.

Planning and preparation involved purchasing gifts for the "tree." A musician was engaged for two or three dollars. The men met to decide who would "go on the door" to collect the admission fees of ten or twenty cents. Others were chosen to sell tickets on the tree or look after the "gun," for target shooting, and games of chance. The women met to plan the cooking and serving of supper. Decisions were made as to who would bring kettles, table cloths, cutlery and dishes. Extra bread was baked and "everything of the best was planned to make a good impression on the out harbour people."

> Then the day of the spree was really a busy one. There were slide loads of dried cut wood hauled to the school to assure a good fire to boil the kettles. Water barrels had to be placed in the school filled for use during the night. Lamps were filled with oil, wicks trimmed and the chimneys cleaned. The men constructed a long table for the meal and the ladies took time in the afternoon to set the tables and make sure there were pans and cloths on hand to wash dishes during the meal time. A special spruce

or fir tree was cut and laden with all the prizes; each prize had a number attached to it. The tree was raised by a long rope and tied to the ceiling to be lowered later on during the night for the prize claiming . . . . The children were caught up in this as well and helped out wherever possible by doing errands and helpful chores.

By late afternoon everyone went home to get ready for the evening:

The ladies had their hair curled and special new dresses, usually home made. Suits were pressed, collars starched and boots polished, and the men looked their best. . . . Some responsible person lit the lamps and the fire. The fiddler arrived early and played a few tunes to get "warmed up."

The women and children arrived promptly, though the men usually stopped at a friend's house along the way for a drink. Although liquor was not drunk in the school, "men went from house to house in groups at intervals and came back to dance." The visiting men from other communities usually joined them for a drink. Although the student comments that "the residents of Tickle Cove were usually well-behaved and were not known to be involved in disturbances or brawls," the observation can only indicate concern about such conflicts.

As soon as a reasonable number of people had gathered in the school, tickets were sold on the prizes that were tied to the "Tree" and raised to the ceiling. This went on throughout the night until about midnight, when the tree was lowered and the prizes claimed.

The school desks were pushed back to the walls to make space for the dancing, which began early in the evening. The Square Dance and occasionally a Virginia Reel were performed.

Some lively dancers would swing a partner so fast that it was a common occurrence to see a girl lifted off her feet or perhaps lose her balance and fall on her knees on the floor.

A supper of the "finest ham butt . . . boiled with cabbage, turnip, carrots and potatoes," was served while the dancing went on. As the women finished their work, they joined in the dancing or sat and watched together with the young children who were still awake. Between the square dances, a step dancer was usually asked to perform a solo single or double step. All would watch and applaud his performance. Occasionally, a singer might receive similar recognition.

Eventually, someone would announce that the last dance would be the Kissing Dance. As one's choice of partner in the dance was often an indication of a choice of beau, "some curious old ladies who had heard rumours of possible courtship would wait around all night to see who asked whom out in the 'Kissing Dance'." The following day the school was rearranged and cleaned by the women:

> While this cleaning was going on there was much to be talked about, how things went, who escorted whom home, and the main topic, "everyone had a good time." The money was counted, the fiddler and any other expenses paid and the proceeds given to the pastor.

Except for the restrictions imposed by the winter weather, the Tickle Cove sprees were identical to the summer garden parties described to me in Plate Cove. Each was a fund-raising event sponsored by the church, organized at the community level and attended by a regional group. The supper and dance were the major activities, and responsibility for them was roughly divided between the men and women. Social drinking was an important aspect of the men's behavior, but was covert and not allowed at the actual scene of the dance.

Throughout the available sources similar activities were found among predominantly Anglican and Catholic communities. In many communities dominated by the United Church, however, where dancing was often forbidden or at least discouraged, it was not a part of the church events. On Fogo Island, for example, the United Church forbade card playing and dancing at their times, in contrast to the events of other religious groups.[26] Likewise in Winterton, Trinity Bay, the United Church garden party allowed no games of chance or dancing. They offered only the supper and a grab bag for children, while Broad Cove, Conception Bay, had only singing and skits.[27]

Communities with large populations of some Protestant denominations often discouraged dancing in general. In

Heart's Ease, Trinity Bay, for instance, opposition was strong to dancing in the United Church school. The day after one dance was held there, a man who lived nearby

> was going around trying to get people all on the go by telling how, "I never got asleep 'till de wee hours of the mornin. Dey was kickin' de old school down. What a racket." He said they were the devil's youngsters and it "shoulden' be allowed."

As a result, the older people "got up in arms" and there was no dancing there for quite some time.[28]

These communities often substituted ring and kissing games in the place of dances.[29] Or, a compromise solution might evolve. In Winterton, Trinity Bay, for example, the young people had to wait until twelve or one o'clock in the morning, when the older people had gone to bed, before they could start any dancing.[30]

These church-sponsored events seem to be continuations of older, more informally organized festivals. The garden parties apparently began in the early years of this century with the encouragement of Roman Catholic and Anglican clergy. Before then, community picnics were held at the end of summer.[31] The Christmas spree is an institutionalization of the informal social activities which generally distinguish that season in Newfoundland tradition.

Fraternal Organizations

Many other dance events were sponsored by formal social organizations, such as the Society of United Fishermen (S.U.F.), the Fishermen's Protective Union (F.P.U.), and the Orange Society. Typically, at such events held in New Perlican, Trinity Bay, during the 1940's, everyone was expected to attend the time.[32] If someone didn't go people wondered "what he had against the crowd," or might comment, "Some nippy, never even went over to have his supper." Despite such verbal sanctions there were still "certain crowds" who went only to their own association's times. The young adults, however, went everywhere.

These events began in the morning as the sponsoring group paraded around the community with their brass band. Visitors then dispersed to private homes to which they had been invited for dinner, and the men would share a few drinks of rum. The afternoon was spent preparing the hall and suppers would be served around 6 o'clock, continuing until all were served, or the food ran out. Typically the fare consisted of a "soup table" and "meat tea," pork and cabbage, and preserves. Tickets were sold for the "draw on the tree," at ten cents each. Cards might be played, unless the event was at the Orange Lodge which did not permit it. After supper a brief concert of hymns and Christmas songs would be presented by the brass band, and finally around 11 o'clock people would begin to say, "Come on now, time to get a dance started or the night is gonna be gone." Once begun the dance continued until the next morning, lasting at times until 6 or 7 o'clock. As one participant commented, "If you lived in the next community and had to walk three or four miles, you were pretty tired by the time you got home, but I've done it. I've often walked five miles after dancing all night."

While there was no charge "on the door," one paid separately for the supper, draw on the tree, and for each dance. A dance was 25 cents and the men were expected to pay for their partners. What was raised on the dance went to pay the fiddler.

As at the garden parties, people always wore their "best bit [sic] and tucker," although as the dance progressed, "the tie would come off, followed by the jacket and then they would roll up their sleeves." There was always a large crowd at the dance and often a rush to get on the floor. The dancers were of all ages from their teens to their fifties, with a majority in their twenties or thirties. Square sets and step dances were performed to accordion music played by a formally hired musician. Not much went on once the dance broke up, "except the usual courting sessions of course . . . after one became of mature age," and when the men gathered the next evening, budding romances were always a popular topic. Drinking and swearing were discouraged in the hall, but were indulged in outdoors by the men.

Fights and so called "rackets" occasionally occurred at these events as well, but people again usually ascribed them to festering conflicts or drunkenness rather than dance related interactions. In response to fights people might comment that, "he had it in when he come here," or, "that's liquor talking." Once in a while, a fight might erupt when partners were chosen by drawing names from a hat and one man danced with another's wife or girlfriend. The offenders however would be put out of the hall for the rest of the night, and in general one could, as I was often told, ask anyone for a dance. The common dissociation of conflict from the dance events which sometimes occasioned it expresses the integrative ideal associated with the old-time dance events.

Tizzard has described in some detail an Orangeman's time which followed the same pattern.[33] But as Salt Pans, New World Islands, Notre Dame Bay, where it took place, was a United Church community no dancing was permitted. Instead games such as "Tucker," "Sir Roger," "musical chairs," and "spin the bottle," were played. The most popular and important game was simply called a "Ring." All but the strictest members of the lodge joined in this performance, which was accompanied by music played on an accordion which was owned by the lodge, and played only for their times.

Organized social groups also sponsored times for their own members, such as those held by the S.U.F. in Change Islands. The lodge by-laws stated the fishermen were allowed three free dances a year in their building, while organizations holding other dances there had to pay a rental fee of $8.00. The lodge dances were held on Candlemas Day, February 2nd, Boxing Day, December 26th, and one other day, usually sometime in the winter when most members would be able to attend.

> On Candlemas day, the day when the fishermen had their "time," the lodge would be filled with members dressed in their regalia. First there would be the supper, which consisted of different dishes each year. The different varieties were bean suppers, soup suppers, or salt meat dinners. . . . After the supper was served the men cleared away the lodge for square dancing. Many times there were three sets going in "full swing". This would cause some complications because the toe tapping of the men would overtop the accordion music. However, to remedy this the members appointed a "floor boss" to make sure all sets

70

were doing the same procedures all the same time and that there wasn't too much shouting.[34]

An informant from Harbour Buffet, Placentia Bay, once commented to me that the "private" lodge dances were always better than the "public" times because of the fewer people in attendance. The dance floor was less crowded and noisy, thus the dancing could be performed with more success and attention to detail. In this way they were similar to the community-only dances which sometimes followed garden parties.[35]

There are similarities among all the events discussed thus far, in addition to the general characteristics of hall times noted earlier. The structure of these events established boundaries between social groups. These groups might be defined by a variety of social relations, such as place of residence, church affiliation or membership in a fraternal organization. The festivals are sponsored by a group which makes the necessary preparations and hosts a larger social group of which it is a part. This larger group in turn supports and recognizes the smaller by its attendance. A community sponsors a time to which residents of nearby places come, a church group holds a fund raiser to which nonmembers come, or the S.U.F. holds a time to which all are welcome. The larger groups are, in fact, expected to attend. Thus, in addition to defining group membership, the events also provide occasion for the maintenance of relations across these boundaries.

Informal Community Festivals

Festival-like dancing events such as those I have been describing were not always organized through formal channels. The Christmas times in Plate Cove for example, did not emphasize church fund raising as did those in Tickle Cove. If held in the school, fees were charged simply to cover expenses. The dance behavior was much the same, but the context less formal. Musicians, instead of being paid a fee, were "paid" with frequent offerings of liquor from the men. As one musician from Harbour Buffet described it:

> They'd all give me some. I'd be playing for them, you know. A drink from this fellow, a drink from that fellow. . . . But I've often been that drunk, you know, that

71

I had to shut my eyes . . . so I wouldn't fall off the chair.[36.]

Mick Keough recalled the Christmas times of his younger days:

> after dinner about three o'clock, 'twould be get out in the big dances. Yes Quotillians [sic], square dances, reels, we used to have. And, anyhow, I used to play the violin and there would be no such thing as anybody else coming to play. There was very good players. "No, wait 'till Keough comes 'cause he can make her speak whatever way we wants her to." Now, very well, we'd dance away then 'till twelve o'clock in the night and all of that.

Although he didn't specify the locale here it seems these were held in the school house. He went on to say:

> and if I was invited to a hall or a school like we have along, you know, "Would I go play?" Oh, I'd go perhaps first most of the time and I'd get in the hall and tune up the violin and I'd start in playing. And by and by you could hear off half-a-mile . . . . Oh yes, yes. That's a silent night. And, "Boys," they'd say, "Keough is in the hall." By and by hear this rushing coming be the hall. "Ah he's in there now. Can make her, the violin [speak]. Yes, can say the words, tunes and songs and everything." And they'd come in and crowd the floor. And now, they knowed how ta keep time and dance too you know. . . . Square dances and reels, quotillians . . . . Oh yes we used to have the kissin' dance the last of it . . . and waltzes.[37]

Cyril Keough recalled the dances of more recent years:

> Most every night there would be a dance in one community, one place, one community another night. Like all around the shore. It would be all square dances then. . . . You'd walk to the dance, go down, and ha, whether it was up or down, whichever place there would be a dance . . . and have the violin playing or someone playing the accordion like that, the square dances. And every now and again you'd be out on those dances, those square dances. . . . And, oh well, you would be sweating then. The water coming out of ya and ya come out by the door. Then probably, be three or four fellers then, your buddies, lined up. They'd have a bottle then come out by the door. Everybody would take out the bottle then and

the moonshine (laugh). Everyone have two or three drinks
out of it and get a cool off and shove the . . . bottle down
in the snow. Like hiding in under the school or
shove him down in through a layer of fence, or if there
was a bit of woods around the school or whatever there
would be. Put the bottle of moonshine down there and
every now and again you'd go out. Every dance you had,
you'd go out and have your drink, two or three drinks out
of your bottle. You'd dance all night then and come home
in the morning. . . . Come home three or four o'clock
soaking from sweat — frost on your clothes — cold in the
house — get in bed to warm it. Then father gets you up
first thing to cut wood — no sleeping in — you'd perish.
By night though you'd be ready to go — keep on for 12
days of Christmas.[38]

It seems there was little change during the years between
these two reports.

In the community of Boxey, on the South Coast, similar
festivities were common. In contrast to the sponsored dances
at which the dancing began relatively late, after the primary
fund-raising activities, the dancing in Boxey began early in
the day. More people of differing ages seemed to participate,
the dances were longer, and the dancing more "lively." More
people of both sexes played accordion as well, and "it was
common to see half a dozen play for a dance." One such
dance is described as follows:

I remember Christmas day . . . they had built a new one
room school in the community but the old one room
school was still there so on Christmas day a crowd of the
young people, older teenagers. . . . and some in their early
twenties got together and went up [to the old school]. We
got an older man up there to play the accordion, . . . I can
see him now with his knee rubber boots on and he standing playing for dear life . . . . So you go home and get
something to eat, and you go up and then in the night
the older married people, the married men and their wives
came along. And there was plenty of St. Pierre rum floating
around. And by and by I smelled this and I couldn't figure
out what this smell was and when I looked they had the
stove . . . and that was red and was lined with salt
caplin . . . . So you would dance away and every now and
then you go along and grab a caplin.[39]

73

The same elements of food and drink exchange, the same occasion, location,and dances previously noted are present in these informal community dance events. Yet there is a relaxation of restrictions found at the more formal sponsored times. Social roles are less specialized. There are many musicians and no floor manager.

Community times of this unsponsored type were held on other calendrical festivals. Saint Patrick's Day, Candlemas, and, possibly, Easter were all observed and celebrated with a dance in Plate Cove.

Mrs. Keough recalled St. Patrick's Day as her family observed it:

> Then St. Patrick's Day would be another big day. . . . My father would get up on the high head of the hall with the violin and my Aunt, when she lived in the other end with her children there, she would get down with the accordion and they'd start playing. And you had to get up then. Supposing it was seven o'clock in the morning, you had to get up. And then you'd have something to eat. Well, everything had to be green.

Mass was attended in the morning, followed by a big meal at home featuring green, lime jelly. By one o'clock in the afternoon:

> we'd all assemble to the school then. There was no parish hall then, which we have now. But, you go to the school, and that was opened up then and there'd be a nominal fee for getting in. Very small, eh. Just for expenditures . . . things have to be got for the school, right . . . there was no electricity here then and you had to have lamps. So you had to buy oil. And then probably a globe would get broken or something like that, wouldn't it father? . . . Probably before the, before one o'clock there'd be a big fight (laugh). The dance was held all evening, right on up to one o'clock. And the minute the clock would strike one o'clock, was like Cinderella, that's it . . . . There'd be so many [at the dance] that you'd be waiting for to get a chance to get on the floor . . . . Sometimes there'd be . . . thirty-two at a time. And then the rest'd be waiting for them to get in, for another crowd, another fresh crowd to get out.

According to Mick, "they'd be pushing for the last dance."[40]

House Times

The house times, hosted by a family and held in their home, contrast with the larger hall times. They were usually seasonal and fairly spontaneous, but were occasionally associated with calendrical observances. They gathered together social groups, defined by the informal networks of kinship, friendship and age group, often referred to as "crowds." The hosting family usually provided the bulk of food and drink, though the guests would usually bring something. This was not formally planned, as at the larger hall functions. A musician or musicians would certainly be invited but not hired and several musicians often took turns playing.

A mouth organ or chin music was commonly used, as well as the accordion or violin. Storytelling and singing were also important at these events. The group dances were performed, but in smaller sets, and step dancing was likely to be more common and less formal, several men perhaps step dancing together.

The house times might be community-wide celebrations in those communities small enough to permit it. Such events would have been similar to the Christmas time described in Boxey, and they are most often reported from the earliest years my sources cover. At that time communities often had no public building or hall, necessitating use of a private house. Occasionally, the owners of houses so used were paid a fee, making the house, in a sense, "public."[41] Thus house times seem to have preceded the more formally organized hall times. They also continued to be important occasions for dancing and had a parallel existence to the hall times, serving the more informal social networks.

Plate Cove people termed these "kitchen times" or "rackets." Mrs. Keough recalled the Candlemas (Calamus) times Mick used to play for as a young man:

> I'll tell you for one thing, Calamus, used to always have what they call the calamus cake, right? . . . The second of February. . . . Two weeks before that they would play cards and whoever lost the game had to make the cake. Isn't that right father? And then, they would have to supply some of the liquor too, eh? And well, they'd, there'd

75

be so many, a lot of 'em playing cards, eh? Then the others would have a drop too, eh? My father would be asked in to play. Although he could dance and sing,you know, but he was the only one at that time then could play you know, and youthful, young for going around, eh? And so they used to have the big dance all night. They'd sing songs and dancing . . . . One year it'd be in one, someone's house, and the next year it would be in a different house, eh? . . . There'd be one end of the kitchen for dancing, one end of the house for dancing, one part, and the next part for eating and drinking. You'd eat in the parlour and dance in the kitchens.[42]

Mick used to play for many of these house times for free.

Such non-institutionally organized house times were common throughout Newfoundland and seem much the same wherever described. An elderly fisherman from Trouty, Trinity Bay, for example, recalled the house times as they were held there:

Before the hall was built, about sixty or more years ago [c. 1910] there were plenty of house times during the winter time. Never had time for dances or any entertainment the rest of the year, we were all too busy with the fishery and our gardens. However, come winter, there was a time in someone's house almost every week. They'd take turns, you know, having dances. In October when the women were berry picking on the barrens, they'd get together over a lunch and decide to have a dance the next week. Square dances was the best fun we had, you know. Perhaps one week, if I came to your house, you'd say, "John, we're having a square dance, a time, Friday night. Tell anyone you see, spread the word around, tell 'em to bring along some vegetables, we'll provide the salt meat, we'll cook a scoff." Next week or so, when you came to my house, I'd tell you we were having a time. The women would get the meal ready, cook the scoff. The rest of us shaped 'er out for a dance. We'd roll up the mats and go to it . . . . About ten o'clock the tables, two or three, would be brought out in the kitchen. They'd serve as many as they could the first time 'round and then serve the rest. They'd clear away the dishes and put the tables back. What feeds some of these were: pork and cabbage, salt beef and cabbage and other vegetables. Rum was cheap then, fifty cents to a dollar a bottle, but it had to be sent out from St. John's by freight or someone in there in the fall by schooner would pick up so much before coming home. You'd never see anyone really drunk though. But we all had a good time. Once the dishes were cleaned off, and the tables put away we'd shape 'er out again. Some old woman would sing for the dance and some of them could certainly sing them jigs. Some of them could really step dance. They'd dance the double. That is a really fast step dance. The music was fast. We danced until daylight, set after set. We'd get home sometimes, change clothes, and take off for the woods. What times![43]

Comments that the priests discouraged the house times are common. Not that they disapproved so much of dancing, rather they wanted the dances to be held under parish auspices. For example, the priest tried unsuccessfully to stop the house times in St. Alban's, Bay d'Espoir, and when Maud Karpeles visited Torbay in 1929, she

did some gate crashing, and went to a private dance at a house which did not belong to the Father's people. It turned out to be a poor affair—a few quadrille figures alternating with an interminable swinging of partners. Some of the guests turned out to be the Father's own people and they were quite discomforted to see him, as he does not approve of private dances, but likes them to be held in the parish hall.[44]

The church and, as we have seen, other institutions, co-opted the social forms of the informal social networks. Their motivation was no doubt partly financial and partly moral, as we have seen the rules of proper decorum more stringently observed at the institutional, hall times. Dancing, however, remained an important social pastime in the context of either milieu, and dance events continued to be held with and without institutional sanction.

Balls

"Balls" or "join(ed) balls," as they were called in Plate Cove, seem to have been a popular social event early in the century. Apparently a formalization of the house times, they are reported from several other communities as well. A number of couples, perhaps under the organization of the

77

schoolmaster, would announce their intention to have a ball and other couples would join for a dollar or two, which would pay for the expenses. In contrast to the community wide celebrations at which all were welcome and even expected to attend, the joined ball was limited to those who had paid. A musician was hired and the owners of the hosting house or parish, if it was held in the school, were paid a nominal fee. According to Mick:

> Well I'll tell you what a ball was. There'd be so many couples get together and, uh, you'd rig out then. Find your kind of stuff and get it all together. And eating and drinking and dancing and reels, cotillions, square dances.[45]

Larry Barker explained that balls in Open Hall were held in the old school, torn down in 1950. The women did not prepare meals for balls, rather the subscription fee was used to buy the food, liquor, and at Christmas a tree with decorations. The teacher, or one couple, would organize this. If there were not enough people in Open Hall, then they'd get people from Plate Cove or Tickle Cove. Larry contrasted these smaller events with the fund-raising times to which everyone came. The dances performed, however, were much the same.[46]

Mrs. Geraldine Keough had saved a damaged newspaper clipping, published 16 February 1900, describing a ball held in her grandfather's house in Plate Cove, which reads as follows:

> Brilliant Ball at Plate Cove
>
> Dear Sir — I beg to chronicle through the columns of your journal, a brief account of a ball given here by Mr. L. Moss on Feb. 2 (Candlemas night). Eighteen couples were invited, and at 6 o'clock all repaired to the scene of festivities. The guests were not a little surprised on entering to behold the magnificent display of decorations with which the rooms were adorned. The ball room especially was
>
> A Veritable Fairyland.
>
> Festoons of evergreen were suspended from all parts of the ceiling, and this combined with the dazzling raiment of the ladies and the light shed by rows of Chinese lanterns, presented a panorama which would form an ideal

subject for the pencil of an artist, and compare favorably with the most of the up-to-date ball rooms of the city. Supper was served at 7 o'clock, and then the music from the ball room offered inducements that few felt inclined to resist. Such an endless succession of reels, quadrills, cotillons, and mazurkas could not fail in chasing away dull care and making the night speed on eagle's wings. The wants of the inner man were attended to many times throughout the night and morn broke, alas! too quickly. At 8 o'clock

"Auld Lang Syne"

was sung and the guests departed, having spent a most enjoyable time.

Those present who contributed songs and other "out harbour guests," from Open Hall and Tickle Cove, are then listed. The women are conspicuously all unmarried and the males include "Mr. J. Long, R.C. teacher, Open Hall." It continued:

Voting for the most popular lady and gentleman was a prominent feature of the entertainment, and Miss L. Cheevers was acknowledged

"Belle of the Ball,"

while Mr. M. Keough carried off the laurels as the most popular gentleman. Your sport from the city would shudder at the idea of spending a winter in one of the more distant outports, but if he had chanced to drop in at "Seaside Cottage" on Candlemas night, and view from an impartial standpoint the many and varied sources of amusement his opinion would be changed considerably, and he would say that grim winter after all has its attractions for the youth of the outport as well as of the city.[47]

While balls are not commonly reported in my sources, there are a few other mentions of them. A memorable "mummers' ball" was held in Tilting, Fogo, in 1906, where "dollar balls" were also popular. At these each guest had to pay a dollar to the "woman of the house." In later years these were held in the parish hall. As in Plate Cove, they featured the choosing of a Belle and Beau.[48]

In Ferryland, balls were held twice yearly; once before Christmas and again in early summer. While more of a community affair than those described in Plate Cove, there are many similarities. The ball was hosted by a family who were paid for the use of their house. Each participant brought a donation of food or drink. Quadrilles were danced during the first part of the evening, often prompted by the owner of the house. A large meal, or scoff, was held about 11:00 p.m., following which "came the most important part of the Ball, the choosing of the Belle and Beau." Usually the couple chosen were young, single people who had never been chosen before. This couple danced a waltz together with the host couple and the couple who assisted them in picking the Belle and Beau. Eventually the crowd broke up in the early morning and the fiddler was paid his fee collected by passing the hat.[49]

Balls are distinguished as formalized non-institutional social gatherings. They are an imitation of urban dance events such as those often described in 19th century dancing manuals.[50] This is clear in the newspaper description of the ball in Plate Cove, which compares it with city practices several times. Suggestions that the teacher was often responsible for organizing these events, and his presence in Plate Cove, additionally suggest an association with the more "sophisticated" society he represented in the outport context.

Weddings

Weddings provided another important occasion for dancing. As usual at "times," the dancing followed the associated social activities, in this case the marriage ceremony. The wedding supper and, more especially, the dance provided an opportunity for those in the community not immediately related to the wedding couple to participate in the celebration. The event was open to all and, though invitations might be sent, once the dance started all were welcome.[51]

At weddings the bride and groom were sometimes recognized in a special dance. In St Lawrence, Placentia Bay, the first dance of the evening would be "Haste to the Wedding." The bride and groom would "head it off" with eight other couples, the bridesmaid and bride's boy. The bride and bridegroom were the first to come on and the last to leave the floor.[52] At a wedding dance in Change Islands the bride was obliged to dance with all the men there before the night was out.[53] The rest of the dance was similar to other community dances featuring group dances, solo performances and waltzes. A collection was taken up for the musician halfway through the night. The dance ended by one or two o'clock, although the party would continue in private houses for the rest of the night. As at most such events, there was always some fighting.

Mumming

The Christmas season, while providing occasion for community times, was also the season for informal house visiting and mumming.[54] The mummers' dancing was loud and often unruly. They often danced with people with whom they would not ordinarily dance when not mummering, and might dance uninvited into the prohibited inner parlour of the house. Dancing on these occasions usually took the form of step dancing which might be used as a means of identifying or concealing the identity of the mummers, as well as allowing mutual participation of both the mummers and household members.[55]

Group dances were not common during the mummers' visits, but might culminate the evening's rounds when the mummers, with their followers collected along the way, arrived at their final stop. In a few Protestant communities, where dancing was not allowed, the mummers played the circle and kissing games we have already encountered.[56]

Cyril Keough recalled the Christmas visiting customs in Plate Cove for his nephew, Bernard, in this way:

> And the next day, then Christmas Day, well you'd go then from one house to the other and that crowd. Singing and dancing, accordions and violins and mouth organs. Singing songs. One crowd would go to your house, you'd go to theirs, go to someone else's and all like that. And have a dance then this place and scuff that place. 'Twas no carpet then, no. Some houses even no canvas or just the hard floor and you'd wallop her down.[57]

Similar customs are found throughout Newfoundland.

One of the more complete descriptions is this from Ferryland and Aquaforte:

> Every year the men or sometimes the men and women did their Christmas visiting. After a few stops, each visit grew larger and the atmosphere became party like. The presence of music determined whether or not the visit became a dancing affair. If a member of the host family played an instrument and the right mood was present, he or she would break it out and play. Accordion and mouth organs were the most popular instruments. . . . The most popular form of dance at a Christmas visit was the step-dance which was primarily a man's dance, even though women could do it, as most of our area is Roman Catholic. These step dances usually occurred when the men were out visiting without their wives. When the wives were present although the step dance was still often done if enough people were present the lances [i.e., lancers] could be done. This gave more people an opportunity to get in on the action.
>
> . . . .
>
> As the later visits drew on the merriment slowly died out, the dancing stopped and a few folk songs and Xmas songs became the order. They sat around the kitchen table, on which sat the bottle or two, and coaxed each other to sing.[58]

Bridge Dances

Descending the scale of formality, we come to more spontaneous outdoor events. These were seasonal, possible only during the mild weather of the summer. Bridge dances were unplanned, though perhaps not unexpected, gatherings of young people on the wooden bridge which could be found crossing the stream which ran through most communities. The wooden surface was well suited to dancing and the young men would often perform step dances and play mouth organ at these gatherings. When women were present there might well be group dancing, though often only fragments of the entire dances were performed. The situation is often recalled as one where dances were first learned and practiced.

The bridge dances in Ferryland and Aquaforte have been described as follows:

Every community had a bridge or two where people gathered on the way home [from a house party] and wasted no time starting up the music again and beginning what is now called, "a dance on the bridge," . . . Bridges were the favorite dance floors because they were such a solid wooden platform on which you could leave no rubber heel marks or tear canvas. As the crowd slowly gathered on the bridge chatting and explaining how good a time they had at a spree, someone would arrive with a mouth organ or accordion and start playing a few jigs, etc . . . . [Or] If a crowd of young people were in the same area on a certain night and there was no other pastime, one of them would play or sing a tune and they all practiced their steps in the cool night air on the bridge. . . . The dances were in no way formal . . . . Square dances and eights were unusual because of the lack of lighting and it was too organized a dance to be done in the dark. It was not uncommon to see two boys on the bridge at night practicing their steps and passing the time.[59]

Wharf Dances

Similar dancing seems to have been common on the other outdoor wooden surface available in most communities. In Port Kirwan, for example, the wharf was used for dances during the summer months, when the hall was unavailable. There might be two a week, which, if fish was scarce, might last until the early morning hours. On Sunday afternoons the young people might dance on the bridge until late afternoon using instruments or gob music. During slack fishing the crowd might then move down to the wharf to be joined by the whole community. According to one source, it was "really a sin to say, [but] everybody was delighted there was no fish," which gave them the opportunity to dance with a crowd of men from Placentia, there fishing for a few weeks.[60]

At the house times and less formal dance events informal social networks gathered together to maintain their relations and celebrate their existence. There was less emphasis on host/guest distinctions than in the organization of hall times. In both types of event though, dance served as a unifying element. While tensions between groups and individuals did not disappear during the dance, they were at least temporarily submerged in the mutual participation and cooperation required for its performance.

Transient Work Scenes

Thus far I have been describing dance events which drew participants primarily from within single communities or vernacular regions. Individuals often moved beyond these boundaries, however, and might participate in dances far beyond their home communities. Sometimes visits from outside a community would actually occasion a dance event. In the late Fall on Fogo Island, for example, schooners on their way back from the Labrador would stop, and dances and suppers were held, attended by the locals and visitors from the vessels.[61] Similar events were held in Bay d'Espoir, Branch, and Petite Forte, when schooners came in from the Banks for bait.[62] These visitors were often from American ships. One informant attended dances all around Newfoundland while working on coastal steamers. He observed that differences between regional dance traditions were noticeable but had enough similarities to allow participation wherever he went. Such differences were one aspect of local identity, while the similarities reflected a unified, pan-Newfoundland culture. As transportation improved during the twentieth century, dance traditions, along with other aspects of outport life, tended toward increased standardization.

Among my Plate Cove informants transient work scenes were an important environment for such out-of-community dancing. Mick Keough went to work in Grand Falls several times and tells many stories of his experiences there. I recorded one about a dance he attended in which he expresses a sense of loyalty to his own ''place,'' and his superiority, as its representative, in dancing. He told it as follows:

> Mrs. Cashin see, she had a store, grocery store. And she turned to and she got a dance hall built onto the store see, where you could go out into the dance hall from the store. But now there was . . . me and another fella, we were . . . shackin' ourselves, cooking for ourselves in a shack. And now the shack belonged to her. She had shacks, you know, for people . . . if they wanted them.

And anyhow, she got this piece onto the old dance hall
and she was going to open it this night see, for to have
a dance. And very well, she said, "Boys," she says, "come
out," she says. Now, we lived about half a mile or
that . . . from the hall. She says, "Boys," she says, "get
ready," she says. "Get your suppers early," she says, "and
come to the dance."

The dancing was formally organized with a floor master in
charge and numbered dances, which one booked at the
beginning of the evening. It seems that even more formal
regulation of behavior is required in this setting than at hall
times and the dancing is clearly less subtle. Mick described
the scene which followed that night as follows:

Be gob, we were booked for the fourth dance see. There
was fellas ahead of us see. And, . . . they knowed nothing
about keeping time, only get out and go on like this, you
know. And another man was saying he was a good fiddler and that's what I was told. And old Jack and I used
to think it a pity the fine tunes that he was [not playing
properly]. So be gar, all right, . . . by and by Mrs. Cashin,
now she was a really good hand in a square dance. There
was a lot of women there. She was about handy sixty-five
then . . . she was a good hand in a dance. So all right, be
gar . . . Mrs. Cashin says, "Jack," she says "you never
had a dance tonight." Jack says, "No ma'am." "My
God," she says, "they're sixth dance now," she says,
"and you were booked for the fourth." . . . Anyhow, all
right, she went to the floor master. She says, "There're
men here never had a dance tonight and they were booked for the fourth dance." "Well," he said, "they couldn't
be around," he says, "cause," he says, "I called out."
And, "Whoa," he says, "boys," he says, "ye got to make
room, to make room for those two men to get out,"
see. . . . And what they done, they all got on one side of
the hall and leave the other side for Jack and me. Jack says
to me, "That's a pretty good show for us," (laugh), I said,
"yeah." And, be gob, the fiddler started with a tune and
away they all goes (laugh). And, well, it come our parts
you know, we just turned to.

As the story continues, the point becomes clear that he and
Jack were good dancers and musicians while the others there
were not:

Alright now, when it comes our part of the first tune, of the first part of the dance, Jack and I just scuffed along you know . . . .And this other fellow now . . . Bill Cross was his name, now, and he belonged down to Tickle Cove see, and I knows him quite well. And anyhow, I said to Bill, I says, "I wonder," I says, "will he hasten the tune a bit?" "Come up," he said. "God," I said, "I don't know." "Yes," he says, come up." I went up and he says, this man said, "The dance up bar," he says, "when it comes to your part," he says, "would you give the tune a little [words obscured]." "Yes boy," he says, "Indeed I will." And all right, we went to our places, And we, dance up, now, when it come our part, we danced. He and I we could keep pretty good time, you know, in dances. And old fiddler says, "Men," he says, "I don't know who ye are," he says, "but by gob," he says, "it is a pleasure," he says, "to play for ye. Ye can keep good time," see. And that killed them altogether (laugh).[63]

Dance Rhymes

Turning from the types of situations for dancing to other aspects of the dance events, I have found that the rhymes associated with dance tunes, are especially revealing. These rhymes were often used along with nonsense syllables to provide a vocal accompaniment for dancing known as chin or gob music. When instrumental accompaniment was used for dancing the rhymes were often interjected by bystanders, both during and between dances, and were occasionally sung by the dancers themselves. One fiddler from the Northern Peninsula recalled for me the verses of a tune known as "The Leg of a Chicken," which he said the dancers would sing in full voice along with his fiddle as they moved through the thread the needle figure:

The leg of a chicken is very good pickin'
The leg of a duck, the leg of a duck
We'll give it to Nelly to stick in her belly
The leg of a duck, the leg of a duck.[64]

Similar rhymes have been reported from throughout Newfoundland and although they may be recited outside the dance event context, as I often heard them in Plate Cove, and used as nursery rhymes or taunts, they are primarily associated with dance music. Musicians and dancers use these rhymes to remember tunes and shortened versions often serve as tune titles. They reflect and augment, on the verbal level, the cultural values enacted in the nonverbal dance forms.

Taunts between communities are common among the collected variants. Two verses often heard to the tune "Mussels in the Corner" refer to the "Dirty Old Torbay Men":

Down the street as thick as flies
Dirty necks and dirty ties,
Dirty rings around their eyes
Dirty old Torbay men.

Ask the bayman for a smoke
He'll just say his pipe is broke
Ask the bayman for a chew
He'll bite it off and give it to you
'Cause he's afraid that you'll take two
Dirty old Torbay man.[65]

Variations on these verses seem almost endless.

Verses might occasionally be used to taunt an individual or family as well. Though the specific references are unclear, the intent is apparent in the following parody:

Did you ever see a Kelly
A going to a rally
With the rounds on his sleeve
Sayin' "God save the King?"[66]

The informant refused to finish the rhyme, not wishing to sing an offensive word for the collector.

The predominant theme among the dance rhymes, however, is sexuality. Most employ innuendo, as in the well known

Chase me Charlie I got Barley
Up the leg of me drawers
If you don't believe it come and see it,
Up the leg of me drawers.[67]

which was the most frequently recalled dance tune around Bay d'Espoir. Or, the following "Cuckoo's Nest" verse:

Some like the girls who are pretty in the face,
Some like the girls who are neat around the waist

But I love the girls with a wriggle and a twist
In the bottom of her belly is the cuckoo's nest.[68]

Sexuality could be rather coarsely expressed, but as as a student from Change Islands noted, some vulgarity was tolerated as ''everyone was out to enjoy themselves.''[69] More explicit variants, often parodies, such as those using obscene language, would more often be sung at night among a crowd of young people courting, rather than at a hall during a dance. The explicit verses also served as sexual taunts shouted between groups of teenage boys and girls on the road.[70] Sexually explicit rhymes are also heard at male gatherings along with other forms of sexual humor.[71]

The social controls on sexuality are acknowledged as in the following stanza I heard in Plate Cove, which is widely reported among the archive sources:

Rowed up in a dory
Came down in a flat
I'm a decent married woman
Take your hand out of that.[72]

Proper courting behavior is emphasized in the following:

The crazy girl that gets a kiss
Goes home and tells her mother
She got to get her lips cut off
And never to kiss another.[73]

As I heard this verse from different people in Plate Cove, the various actors' slots could be filled by either sex, but all versions agreed that kissing should remain a private affair.

While most rhymes found in the dance context use sexual innuendo, what they are suggesting is perfectly clear. Even when they were not sung at dances, most participants knew the rhymes and could not help but recall them upon hearing their associated tunes. One man commented that he would become embarrassed just hearing the tunes, much less their rhymes.[74] In my experience, crucial lines are often omitted or obscured in performances, yet the audience still responds with gales of laughter and appreciative howls. Obviously, they recognized and knew the rhyme, even though I did not. Thus, even when not sung, the association of those traditional rhymes with particular tunes would bring them to mind and contribute to the already highly charged atmosphere of the dance event. Altogether, these rhymes reflect at least some of the functions of dance events, which, along with others, are also enacted in the dances themselves, the organization of the events, and their associated behaviors.

Dance Descriptions

Descriptions of the dance events at which group dances were performed often emphasize their integrative goals. Dancers usually describe their dance experience metaphorically through those elements they choose to recount. They recall the length of dances, the fatigue of the dancers, the smell and the sweat. One informant, for example, described the community dances as follows:

> As the dance progressed the tie would come off, followed by the jacket and then they would roll up their sleeves. Between sets you'd head for the front steps and you'd see the steam flying. Only the men went outside and they didn't seem to mind the cold apparently as it was "all considered part of the dancing." . . . After the dance was well underway, the sweat would begin to show on the participants and the odors would come through. But this wasn't as strong then as it is today, as most people wore home spun knitted clothing which absorbed the moisture somewhat. "Some of the lads with the home spun underwear used to have some trouble with the underwear shrinking."[75]

This speaker is eager to describe the type of intimacy achieved during the dance event. This is apparent in his description of progressive deshabille during the dance; a motif he often employed to emphasize an increase in the dancers' involvement as the dance progressed. The attitudes toward "sweat" and "odor" implicit in his comments reinforce the image of a personal level of intimacy. The crowded setting of the dance and the physical exertion required in the performance helped to create an environment in which a relatively large group of people became increasingly more physically intimate as they all got hot together.

Immersion of the individual in a euphoria created by the dance is a phenomenon commonly reported. Wilf Doyle, a well-known dance musician, for example, commented that during the Lancers the dancers "became so caught up in their dancing that for the next half hour their bodies were slaves to the music."[76] We should recall the emphasis on alcohol consumption at virtually all dances, and consider the contribution of mild intoxication to the dancers' experience. The high level of sensory stimulation at dance events probably tends to increase the impact of the dance on the participants.[77]

Dance Movement

Newfoundland dancing, as we have seen, places a strong emphasis on abstract floor design and individual rhythmic, or occasionally, gestural articulation. One can examine the significance of the floor patterns at several levels: the whole performance as a single entity; the discursive performance, that is its progress from beginning to end; and, specific movements within the dance. The body action of individual dancers is another level, important in the solo dances as well as the group dances.[78] The meaning of movements within the dances can be examined in relation to the everyday patterns of nonverbal behavior. Proxemic codes (the socially determined amounts of space people maintain between themselves and others) are particularly relevant to the significance of floor design and dance organization. Each organizational form (individual, couple, or group) reflects a different nonverbal communicative structure: individual display before an audience; mixed-sex coupling; or, an emphasis on group interactions. Each enables the participants to experience a different set of relationships through which they may pursue their personal goals and in which the dances' social functions are achieved.

During a dance an involvement sufficient to sustain the dance performance is required of the dancers.[79] Dancers are free to make use of the usual means of interpersonal communication available in everyday interaction, but the dance performance requires involvement in a prescribed set of relationships. Dancers may participate reluctantly and communicate this to the other participants, but they must be involved if the dance is to continue at all. It is on the significance of the obligatory relationships that I base my following analysis of the dance patterns.

While a similar dance tradition is employed at all the dance events I have discussed thus far, the forms emphasized vary among the different situations. Organization of the dancing ranges from the group dances interspersed with solo Step Dance performances, which was once typical of all public occasions, known as "hall times," through group dances performed in smaller sets with step dancing performed more often by several men at once, which was typically found at smaller dance events such as the "house times," to freely organized step dancing and couple swinging, which was common during the most spontaneous and smallest gatherings, such as the bridge dances, mummers' visits and other occasions too loosely structured to have names.

The courtship goals frequently referred to by dance participants are found expressed at several levels. The division of dancers into male and female roles, for example, is the most significant and universal distinction in the movement style of individual dancers. These contrastive movement patterns are "metaphors for social roles."[80] The men are expected to dance vigorously while the women, often described as "lackadaisical," watch and, one assumes, admire the men. Men usually take the active role in partner choosing. The formal reversal of these roles is even identified as a distinct dance, the Ladies' Privilege.

The distinction between male and female roles is also central to the structure of the group dances. Many specific movements, or figures, within these dances involve mixed-sex coupling. Swinging, for example, is a secondary figure which permeates all the group dances. It is the most intimate relationship established, and is created proxemically as the dancers embrace one another. They can feel, smell, and see one another at close range. Visual, thermal, and olfactory codes come into play; all of them reinforcing the perception of intimacy. Several of the figures in which the individual men and women perform as separate groups emphasize this role distinction as well. "Ladies in," for example, separates the two groups, while "exchange partners" figures, such as "round the house," mix the two groups together as individuals.

Couple dancing, while integral to the group dances, is also found as a choreographic form in its own right. These dances, primarily the waltz, are, however, infrequently reported from events at which group dances were performed. It seems group dances sufficiently met the need for this communicative structure.

Partner choosing games, such as the Kissing Dance, are the most elaborate courtship enactment in the dance repertoire. The specific movement of kissing is a "dramatic pantomime," of courtship concerns.[81] The group figures of the dance are the "ladies in" and "right and left" which also reflect the distinction between male and female roles. The final figure is once again a partner swing; the most intimate coupling in the repertoire of specific movements.

As a whole performance, the Kissing Dance may be seen to enact the courtship concern which runs throughout the dance event. It is always reported as the last dance of the event, undoubtedly the most important coupling of the event, as testified by the reported interest of the old women of Tickle Cove in who danced with whom. Formalization of this function in the playfully ritual motions of the Kissing Dance protected the participants at the moment of high social risk, although their import might be acknowledged by all.

Display and competition are themes frequently expressed in descriptions of male dancing. These are closely related to sexual concerns, and thus step dancing in the group dances frequently precedes or follows swinging. During these minor movement units the men will try to "outdance" one another in a competitive display.

The egocentric display of step dancing is also an expression of friendly, or not so friendly, rivalry among the men. As an independent form, step dancing was commonly associated with male dominated gatherings such as those on shipboard, called forecastle times, or on community bridges. It reached its most formal expression as a competitive form at the regional gatherings. In these contexts it probably reflected inter-community as well as courtship-based rivalry.

The cooperative ethos of the dance events is enacted primarily in the group dances. Many of the specific movements within them integrate the dancers in a cohesive performance unit. Group figures such as the circle symbolize this most clearly. In the discoursive performance of the group dances as well, the integration of individual dancers into a communal entity is made physically apparent.

The Square Dance, in particular, employs this discoursive mode of progressive integration. It begins as a group of couples. These couples are formed into pairs and eventually the whole is welded together. Then the original pairings are broken down and everyone's mutual membership as man or woman in the community of dancers is affirmed.

This progression is most clearly seen in the distinctive figures. The secondary figures, on the other hand, enact couple relationships, in swinging, or individual display, in step dancing. These secondary relationships are set within the framework provided by the sequential performance of distinctive figures.

In the first part of the Square Dance, in which dancers cross the set singly or as couples, the facing couples acknowledge each other as dance partners, but do not yet interact too closely. This bar is a preliminary interaction between the facing couples which stresses, primarily, the couple relationships, gives the men a chance to show off, and begins the dancers' progressive surrender to the imperatives of the dance and music. When this introductory section of the dance is performed in two parts, there is often a progression from single crossing or couples passing by to an arch movement. "Going under" an arch demands more mutual attention and coordination of effort among the dancers than simply "passing by." Nonverbal cues must be consciously sent and carefully observed for the successful performance of these movements.

In "form a line" the facing couples link hands and form a larger unit within the dance. Touch is introduced beyond the original partner linkage, and individuals begin to interact intimately with persons other than their own partner.

"Take two," carries this progression a step further as each man has the opportunity to relate intimately with both women at once. Significantly, the single man simultaneously does his best to attract attention with a display of step dance prowess. The secondary figures may become more intimate as well, as couples "step dance" and cross the set, not hand in hand, but in a closed embrace.

In the final section the dancers join together as one group, though still coupled with their partners. They "close in," increasing their proxemic sense of intimacy and may circle as a group. The pairing of original couples is broken down and the women and men may both perform *en masse*, as in "ladies in." The relationship is now not so much between individual men and individual women, but rather between the men and women as groups. Similarly in the exchange partner figures, the original couples are separated and individuals are mixed together. The dancers perform as individual male or female entities within the larger social group.

Although the Lancers' figures differ from those of the Square Dance, their progression is equivalent. The dance begins with similar couple interactions, but moves more quickly to group figures. As in the Square Dance, some figures, such as the "longways reel," separate the men and women into groups. Others, such as the "basket" and "thread the needle," unite the dancers in a single group formation.

The Reel employs a similar repertoire of figures and relationships, but places less emphasis on their progressive sequence. The Reel begins with both "all join" and "exchange partner" group figures, interpolating two couple interactions — swinging and solo stepping — throughout. There is some sense of progression in the couple interactions: the first figure involves a two couple relationship; the second mixes the individual men and women; in the third, one couple moves through the entire floor space of the set; and in the final figure each man leads a "thread the needle." Between each, however, is the exchange partner group figure "grand chain."

Conclusion

The choreographic forms found in traditional Newfoundland dance culture seem to symbolize distinctive social roles, their relations, and an idealized communal social ethos. These are expressed in dance formation and structure, contrastive movement styles, discoursive performance, and particular movements. The dances employ proxemic codes to enact these functions. Each is given choreographic expression in a particular dance form, but all are subsumed within the group dances, the special function of which is the pursuit of integrative goals among groups of dancers. This ethos may also be seen in the differences between local versions of the same dance which are perceived as always a bit different in each place. The emphasis placed on these relatively minor distinctions reflects the informants' identification with their place of residence. The whole performance, then, helps to unite a region which shares the same dance forms.

Traditional dance events in rural Newfoundland were enactments of the cultural conceptions of community organization, which channeled sexuality in acceptable ways. At these occasions individuals were allowed license and cathartic release was achieved and expressed through dance. The structure of the dances provides a framework in which the norms are made visible and through which dancers "let off steam" while affirming their allegiance to the cultural order.

NOTES — CHAPTER 3

1. Roger Abrahams, "Towards an Enactment-Centered Theory of Folklore," in *Frontiers of Folklore*, ed. William Bascom (Boulder, Colorado: Westview Press, 1978), pp. 79, 85, 100-01; Joann Kealiinohomoku, "Theory and Methods for an Anthropological Study of Dance," Diss. Indiana University, 1976, pp. 61, 63; Anya Royce, *The Anthropology of Dance* (Bloomington and London: Indiana University Press, 1977), p. 27.

2. Judith Lynne Hanna, "Toward Semantic Analysis of Movement Behavior: Concepts and Problems," *Semiotica,*25 (1978), 77-110; and, *To Dance is Human. A Theory of Nonverbal Communication* (Austin and London: University of Texas Press, 1980), pp. 41-44.

3. Joann Kealiinohomoku, "Dance Culture as a Microcosm of Holistic Culture," in *New Dimensions in Dance Research: Anthropology and the Dance,* ed. Tamara Comstock (New York: Committee on Research in Dance, 1974), p. 99.

4. Hanna, *To Dance is Human*, p. 238.

5. *Dictionary of Newfoundland English*, pp. 568-569.

6. James Faris, *Cat Harbour*, Newfoundland Social and Economic Studies, No. 3 (St. John's: Institute for Social and Economic Research, Memorial University of Newfoundland, 1972), pp. 157-63.

7. The term "crowd" is a flexible one often applied to a group of people at a time. In general use it describes a "group of people, ideally with the same surname and occupants of the same garden or group of gardens, who may be linked in a common economic endeavor. It is a territorial concept, but cannot be divorced from the kinship reference." Faris, pp. 65-67.

8. Wilfred Wareham, "Social Change and Musical Tradition," M.A. Thesis, Memorial University of Newfoundland, 1972, pp. 86-87.

9. Laurel Doucette, "Folk Festival: The Gatineau Valley Church Picnic," *Culture & Tradition*, 1 (1976), 55-62; a similar event from Prince Edward Island is described in Edward Ives, *Lawrence Doyle: The Farmer Poet of Prince Edward Island,* University of Maine Studies, No. 92 (Orono, Maine: University of Maine Press, 1971), pp. 22-24.

10. George Casey, "Traditions and Neighborhoods: The Folklife of a Newfoundland Fishing Outport," M.A. Thesis, Memorial University of Newfoundland, 1971, p. 320.

11. Casey, pp. 310-11.

12. MUNFLA, Ms., 81-271/pp. 88-99.

13. MUNFLA, Q71B-3/p. 7; a similar practice is reported from Fogo as well, MUNFLA, Tape, 72-107/Cll27.

14. MUNFLA, Ms., 81-271/p. 90.

15. MUNFLA, Ms., 81-271/p. 58.

16. MUNFLA, Ms., 81-271/p. 61.

17. MUNFLA, Ms., 81-271/p. 88.

18. MUNFLA, Ms., 81-271/p. 166.

19. MUNFLA, Ms., Q71B-5/p. 13.

20. MUNFLA, Ms., 77-112/p. 55.

21. MUNFLA, Ms., 81-271/pp. 73-74.

22. MUNFLA, Ms., 81-271/p. 176.

23. MUNFLA, Ms., 78-71/p. 18; Kevin Philpott, "The Importance of the Community Wharf in the Social and Economic Life of Plate Cove East," Ms., No. 33 in the Archive of Undergraduate Research on Newfoundland Society and Culture, Memorial University of Newfoundland.

24. Casey, p. 316.

25. The description of sprees is paraphrased and quoted from Cecilia Tracey, "Sprees in Tickle Cove, Bonavista Bay," Ms., No. 438 in the Archive of Undergraduate Research on Newfoundland Society and Culture, Memorial University of Newfoundland.

26. MUNFLA, Ms., 77-283/p. 83.

27. MUNFLA, Q71B-6/p. 15.

28. MUNFLA, Ms., 68-4/pp. 51-52.

29. See for example, Tizzard, pp. 228-29; MUNFLA, Ms., 75-25/p. 14.

30. MUNFLA, Ms., 79-630/p. 5.

31. Tizzard, pp. 254-56.

32. The following description is condensed and quoted from MUNFLA, Ms., 79-630, which was compiled with the aid of a questionnaire guide I prepared for others' use.

33. Tizzard, pp. 228-29.

34. MUNFLA, Ms., 73-75/p. 5.

35. MUNFLA, Ms., 80-41/pp. 9, 15.

36. MUNFLA, Ms., Tape, 79-54/C4108.

37. MUNFLA, Ms., 81-336/pp. 7, 23.

38. MUNFLA, Ms., 81-336/p. 83.

39. MUNFLA, Ms., 79-630/pp. 19-23.

40. MUNFLA, Ms., 81-281/pp. 82-86.

41. For example see MUNFLA, Ms., 77-334/p. 4.

42. MUNFLA, Ms., 81-271/pp. 81-82.

43. MUNFLA, Ms., 73-147/pp. 15-16.

44. MUNFLA, Ms., 74-46/p. 28; MUNFLA Ms., 78-003/folder 7, p. 4.

45. MUNFLA, Ms., 81-271/p. 80.

46. MUNFLA, Ms., 81-271/pp. 164-65.

47. "Brilliant Ball at Plate Cove," *Evening Telegram*, 16 February 1900, (p. 3), col. 3.

48. MUNFLA, Tape, 72-113/C1131.

49. MUNFLA, Ms., 77-155/pp. 15-19.

50. See for example, Elias Howe, *Howe's Complete Ballroom Handbook* (Boston: Elias Howe, 1858); or John M. Schell, *Prompting: How to Do It* (1890; rpt. New York: Carl Fischer, 1948).

51. See for example the discussion of weddings in Faris, pp. 157-60.

52. MUNFLA, Ms., 72-124/p. 13.

53. Personal communication from John Widdowson, 11 August 1981. This wedding was recorded by him as well, MUNFLA, Tape, 65-17/C161-62.

54. The following are indispensable sources of information on these customs: Herbert Halpert and G.M. Story, eds., *Christmas Mumming in Newfoundland* (Toronto: University of Toronto Press, 1969); and Margaret Robertson, "The Newfoundland Mummers' Christmas House-Visit," M.A. Thesis, Memorial University of Newfoundland, 1979, pp. 114-18.

55. See Louis Chiaramonte, "Mumming in 'Deep Harbour'," in *Christmas Mumming in Newfoundland*, ed. Herbert Halpert and G.M. Story (Toronto: University of Toronto Press, 1969), p. 87, for an excellent description of step dancing during a mummers' visit.

56. See for example, MUNFLA, Ms., 78-186/pp. 46-47.

57. MUNFLA, Ms., 81-336/p. 71.

58. MUNFLA, Ms., 77-155/pp. 26-28

59. MUNFLA, Ms., 77-155/pp. 23-25.

60. MUNFLA, Ms., 77-334/pp. 29, 32.

61. MUNFLA, Ms., 77-283/p. 30.

62. MUNFLA, Ms., 74-46/p. 18; Ms., 77-149/p. 15; Ms., 81-271/p. 294.

63. MUNFLA, Ms., 81-271/pp. 94-97.

64. MUNFLA, Ms., 81-271/p. 436.

65. MUNFLA, Folklore Survey Cards, 68-5/54.

66. MUNFLA, Tape, 66-25/C318.

67. MUNFLA, Ms., 74-46/p. 21.

68. MUNFLA, Tape, 79-194/C512.

69. MUNFLA, Ms., 73-75/pp. 7-8.

70. See MUNFLA, Ms., 73-75/pp. 7-8, 11-12.

71. See MUNFLA, Ms., 81-271/pp. 51-55; Tape 81-271/C5194, for my record of such a gathering in Plate Cove.

72. MUNFLA, Ms., 81-271/p. 25.

73. MUNFLA, Ms., 81-271/pp. 25, 51.

74. Personal communication from Herbert Halpert, May 1981.

75. MUNFLA, Ms., 79-630/pp. 12-14.

76. MUNFLA, Ms., 80-118/p. 33.

77. Thomas F. Johnston, "Alaskan Eskimo Dance in Cultural Context," *Dance Research Journal*, 7 (1975), 2.

78. Hanna, *To Dance Is Human*, pp. 41-44.

79. Erving Goffman, *Behavior in Public Places: Notes on the Social Organization of Gatherings* (New York: The Free Press, 1963), p. 196.

80. Hanna, *To Dance Is Human*, p. 91.

81. Hanna, *To Dance Is Human*, p. 41.

CHAPTER FOUR: The Dynamics of Change

The interpretation of dance forms as expressions of social relationships and cultural values is not a new idea. This approach has even been applied occasionally to folk dances of the British-derived North American tradition. Colonial dances in America have been interpreted as reflective of the participants' various social identities.[1] The square dance has been said to suggest the American fascination with process, and been described as symbolic of the dancing ''community of couples,'' as well as reflective of the social networks which bring them together.[2]

While the functions of dance as an expressive form have often been summarized in a general way, the interconnection between specific dance forms and their functions has been less often addressed.[3] Most such interpretations are based on analogies between impressionistic responses to the dance forms and other types of social organization. Drawing on concepts of nonverbal communication, I have illustrated specific means by which dance movement serves its functions, embodies social relationships, and communicates the cultural values which are enacted in the dance events. Change in any aspect of dance culture is bound to have repercussions throughout this expressive system. The observable changes of form and context in Newfoundland dance culture during the first half of the 20th century are explicable as the integrated responses of an expressive system to many changes in the society which it served. As the size and complexity of communities increased, dance forms placed more emphasis on the discursive integration of couples.

The Reel, for example, apparently disappeared as dance events became larger and more dancers had to be accommodated. It is reported from small dance event contexts, such as house times in the small and isolated community of Harbour Deep or the older dance events in other communities, but is seldom mentioned as occurring in larger group contexts such as the garden party or other hall times. The sets performing the Reel were of necessity small ones. Its choreographic structure is not well suited to expansion. An increase of only a few couples would extend the duration of the dance considerably. The Square Dance form, in contrast, could accommodate large numbers with no increase in duration.

Not only would the duration of the large Reel set be unreasonable, the floor space required would be extravagant and large numbers of dancers would be idle during the couple figures. In the Square Dance the same floor space was made to accommodate twice the number of dancers who could actually use it at once by alternating between the end and side couples. The duration of each sequence was sufficient for the dancers to reach full involvement while performing, and then take a short rest, during which attention to the dance was not required at a high level. More rapid alternation between ends and sides is found in smaller sets, such as those described in the Tack's Beach Square Dance, or the Lancers, but dancers had then to remain involved in the dance, taking up space, even when not actively performing. In a large Reel dancers would need to be similarly involved, though physically idle.[4]

One of the most common observations people made when recalling the older dance traditions was their long duration. Although reported as lasting from one-half to a full hour, when performed without long pauses between the parts, the Square Dance and the Reel actually last closer to twenty minutes. This discrepancy may reflect a more relaxed performance style in the older dance events with longer pauses. It may also be an exaggeration meant to emphasize the degree of involvement in the dance performance, much like comments on the dancers' fatigue and perspiration. The modern dances are, however, much shorter in duration, and such informant comments are also meant to highlight this contrast.

There may well be a general historical trend to shorten dance duration. Several versions of the Square Dance were reported in which only two sides of the set were used, eliminating essentially half the dance. In one version I have seen which uses this formation, no breaks were taken between the performance of the facing couple figures, shortening the dance even further. An informant commented on this occasion that they had at one time used the more typical "end" and "side" couple formation with breaks between parts, but this had changed after the Second World War. He couldn't tell me why, except to say that the change made the dance go faster.[5]

The Kissing Dance has also undergone abridgement within my informants' memories. The repetition of the partner choosing sequence was eliminated, and once the chain was formed group figures were performed. This change emphasizes the discoursive expression of progressive integration over the courtship pantomime.

As the dance traditions moved from the house to the hall, there was a restructuring of the dances to accommodate more participants The discoursive performance became the primary level through which this larger group was integrated in the final group figures of the Square Dance and Lancers. In Plate Cove, the Kissing Dance as well was adapted to this discoursive structure, which became the dominant structural form among the folk dances of Newfoundland during the first half of the 20th century.

New Dances at New Events

The dancing one is most likely to observe in a Newfoundland outport today, however, is very different from that which I have described thus far. The group dances have been replaced by the mixed-sex, couple dancing to country or rock music, typically found throughout most of North America. There are two basic forms: the open position, with partners rarely touching, and, closed, with partners often tightly embracing one another, usually performed to fast or slow music respectively.[6]

These dances are performed, as well, in contexts different from the dance events already described. The most common contemporary dance event is simply a "dance," usually sponsored by a club to attract business. On the Bonavista peninsula, and probably elsewhere, these include both "teenage" and "adult" dances, usually held on consecutive nights of a weekend. Teenage dances are for those under the drinking age of nineteen, where no liquor is served. However, young single people and married couples predominate at the adult dances as well. Participants at both will travel outside their communities and even immediate regions to attend. One Saturday night I picked up some adolescent boys hitchhiking up to fifteen miles home to Princeton and Sweet Bay from a teenage dance at Brennan's, a club midway between Plate Cove and Summerville.[7] Young adults of drinking age travel even further in cars, ranging all over the Bonavista Peninsula.

The Transition

Between the dance culture previously described and the new dances and dance events, which have eclipsed the older traditions, there occurred a rather abrupt transition which is difficult to document. Neither archive sources, which tend to focus on the "old times" or the present day, nor my own informants provided much information on dance practice between the two periods.

A common explanation given by informants for the decline of the older dance traditions during the 1950s is that there was a lot of American influence during the 1940s, and Newfoundlanders had begun to travel more as well, which introduced people to other types of dancing. Different types of music became popular as well, made available on radio, juke boxes, and some hi-fi's. It became difficult to get anyone to play music for the older dances. People wanted to throw off their "rustic" image:

> Nobody wanted to be associated with it, we wanted to be more cosmopolitan. We became a part of Canada, our isolation seemed to go and I believe [because of] the overwhelming need to be absorbed, to be considered as part of the continent, a part of the whole as you will, anything which designated us . . . rustic people was not accepted.[8]

The image of a clean and abrupt break with the past and the importance given here to media dissemination and validation of the new forms is typical. This image has some validity if one looks only at the dance forms themselves. As a part of the dance culture I have been describing, however, they could not change independently of their performance contexts. Change in any aspect of the dynamic system of dances, dance events, and the cultural order they enact, related through the communicative nature of dance, is, as I have said before, bound to have repercussions throughout. Recent changes in Newfoundland dance are not simply an abandonment of the older dance forms, but rather a reorientation of the expressive role of dance in society.

A few clearly transitional scenes are documented in my sources and I will draw on one in particular, which describes dances in communities around St. John's in the 1950s, as an example.[9]

These weekly dances were the main social event of the week for the young people who attended. The participants included a majority of young, single men and women, as well as some older men, both single and married, and young married couples who used to attend before their marriage. The young people came from a large area around St. John's and often travelled by car to attend, though there was always a "core group" of locals in each community where such dances were held. The woman who recalled these dances lived in "a loosely populated area outside the city limits, but not within community boundaries," and attended dances in Torbay and, less frequently, Portugal Cove and the Goulds. The latter dances were attended on special occasions, such as a garden party. She was not an "insider" at any of these dances, but was known and had many friends, especially in Torbay. Her socializing with this "crowd," however, was largely limited to the dance events and weekend visits "to meet and talk with friends."

This situation is not unlike the one I found around Plate Cove. The significant difference from the "old time" events seems to be the increased mobility among the participants. The availability of cars to travel further afield was as important in the Torbay area then as it is today in Plate Cove. It seems that the large area thus made accessible results in less closely knit social groups at dance events. This change took place at different times in different areas of the Province depending upon when improvements were made to the roads. The effect of such changes varied in degree as the relative distance between communities is greater in some areas than others. The eventual impact, however, seems to have been much the same in the areas I have visited.

Before the improvement of transportation most large

inter-community gatherings, where young people could meet prospective mates from outside their immediate communities, were held in the context of festival occasions which served several social needs. Among these events I found the enactment of a communal ethos and the culturally sanctioned expression of sexuality to be paramount. The function of the modern dance events, in contrast, has become primarily to provide courtship opportunities. The impact of this change is apparent in the informant's description of her experiences at the dance which emphasizes the young women's strategies to "catch the eye" of the men, and procure a congenial partner for the ride home following the dance. While an eligible young woman at the older dance event might recall similar concerns, the heavy hand of parental presence and community chaperonage served to subdue their expression and necessitated the use of protective ritualized forms such as the Kissing Dance.

The dances most commonly performed at the transitional events were recalled as the waltz, one step, jive, and two step, all mixed-couple dances performed to "modern" music played by a hired band. These forms, however, were adapted by the dancers to fit their sense of propriety and satisfy their expressive needs. They are described as follows:

> Couples held each other while they did these dances, but the partners were allowed to hold each other only so close. If a couple started dancing too close, everyone on the floor would stop dancing and look at them. Thus a couple could not get away with being too intimate in public because everyone was watching what everyone else was doing.

Not only were the new forms somewhat restricted by existing norms, they were also changed to express relationships not inherent in their structure. People felt free to improvise on these couple dances in order to include their friends. Often a couple would start waltzing or doing a two step and grab onto another couple or two. Each person would execute the basic steps but as many as four or more people might be strung together holding hands, kicking their feet up together.

The group forms survived in this context although in slightly changed form. The Lancers was performed when the hired band, who played music "from the radio," took a break. A local, unpaid "accordion player and singer" would then take the stage and provide music. The sense of group integration implied by the groups of waltzing couples was here dominant, explicit and more clearly articulated. Everyone joined in the Lancers and for many of the older people it was the only dance in which they would take part. Not only did they probably feel more comfortable with the dance forms with which they had grown up, but without a strong courtship interest of their own, the Lancers would have been the only dance to provide the dance experience they desired.

The musician played traditional dance tunes while the singer, in actuality a "caller," prompted the figures. Despite this practice, each set had one or more experienced dancers who

> shoved the less experienced into position. The resulting dance was not meant to be a perfect example of this type of dance, but was a dance in which everyone who wanted to could get on the floor. The Lancers might continue for an hour if everyone was in the mood. Once the Lancers started none of the people were allowed to leave the floor or break the set. When the Lancers finished everyone usually went outside to cool off and the hired band resumed playing listening music or modern dance music.

The description of this performance is an encapsulation of the old time dance event ethos: "everyone who wanted" could dance; it lasted a very long time; it required all the dancers' involvement; and, it got everyone very hot.

The basic movements remain much the same as those described earlier. The dance begins with facing couple figures and continues with a longways figure and variation of "thread the needle." The "basket" figure, however, was recalled as the climax of the dance. It is described as follows:

> Another sequence . . . was for everyone to form a circle, so that every woman was between two men. Everyone would then hold hands behind the next person's back so the circle was locked . . . [and] then side step to the music. The object of this was for every man to swing the girl next to him off her feet. The circle would go around faster, until the set finally ended when someone lost hold and a few girls went flying through the air.

What is described as the men's vigorous, "manly behavior" has overwhelmed the dancers' cooperation and effectively ended the dance. This behavior went so far that

> even when the couples were dancing singly the men tried to swing the girls up in the air. When the men were rather drunk they used to drop the girls regularly. My mother said she usually went home with several cuts and bruises.

Instead of the subjection of the individual to the imperatives of the dance movements, with status awarded those who could "keep good time," the dancers seem here to struggle against the form. Instead of a progressive unification culminating in the group figures "right and left" or "thread the needle," the set literally flies apart at its climax. The form is not able to unite the disparate individuals, who are no longer members of a close knit, residential community celebrating their corporate identity in the dance event. The solo step dance form did not survive in this new context at all. The only men who gave such performances were those considered "drunk." The women felt such a man was "making a fool of himself." Drinking was considered appropriate behavior and was expected of the men. Fights broke out frequently and

> the combatants had to go outside and often attracted a number of spectators from those who stepped out to cool off. Fighting was accepted by the participants as being a part of the general excitement.

While male interactions continued to involve drinking, now beer consumed in their cars, and fighting, the structured dance expression of their rivalry — the competitive solo step dance — was not maintained. It seems that the men no longer required a formally sanctioned opportunity for such egocentric display, but rather could indulge themselves at will. These were not men with important social ties outside the dance context; they could afford to fight more openly. In the dance men displayed their "strength and agility . . . by swinging the girls off their feet." Their primary interest was in impressing the women, which they did, sometimes quite physically.

Eventually, perhaps as the dancers still familiar with the older forms aged and stopped attending dances, the group dances ceased to be performed altogether. Contemporary dance forms continue to reflect these changes in the dance event contexts and, while styles follow mass media trends with some time lag, the mixed-sex couple dances are now almost the sole surviving form of purely social dance.

Old Dances at Old Events

Older dance forms still persist in some of the traditional event contexts. House visiting and parties survive as a form of social gathering, especially during the Christmas season. As was the case in former times, singing and instrumental music is often performed at these events along with informal step dancing. The performance of group dances is apparently rare. Gerald Quinton reported playing at several such house parties during the Christmas season of 1980-81.[10] Similar events may occur more spontaneously throughout the year, especially on Friday and Saturday nights. These are often all male gatherings, such as one which took place at the end of my field work in Plate Cove.

This gathering continued throughout the weekend, moving from a local house first to the club in Plate Cove West and later to Brennan's, the much larger club just down the road towards Summerville. We stayed at Brennan's drinking, playing and singing until about two or three o'clock in the morning.

I expected that this would be the end of the party but after Mass on Sunday morning, a number of the crowd gathered again at Brennan's and continued to drink, sing, and play music. Several men were there from Stock Cove and although the two groups sat at different tables, each listened to the other's performances. The "juke box" was occasionally played by other patrons, but ignored by the performers and their listeners. I eventually had to leave, although the gathering did not seem to be ending. Step dancing was not a prominent part of the entertainment, but was performed by a local man known for his ability as a dancer, after sufficient coaxing from "the boys." It was recognized as an appropriate performance genre in that situation.[11]

Some informal social gatherings self-consciously emphasize the older performance traditions. Many of the social gatherings that I participated in were influenced by this attitude because of my expressed interest in these forms. Others were reported to me. I know of one instance during my stay when Gerald was invited to a house party specifically as a musician because some of the host's relatives were visiting from the States and wanted to hear the old music. He seemed to imply this was a common occurrence.[12]

Similarly, an informant from Conception Harbour commented that the "Yanks," meaning Newfoundlanders who emigrated to the United States, return every summer and always want to do the Lancers. In that community a garden party and parish dances are held during the summer months which cater to that group and at which the Lancers is danced.[13]

The older forms of music and dance have become identified with a conception of Newfoundland cultural identity which is particularly important to those who have left. Newfoundlanders in mainland Canada are reported to perform a dance in longways formation, as follows:

> Each couple in turn, starting from the top will dance "free style" (a figure or step of their choice) down the middle from top to bottom of the set as those on the side clap hands and move up to maintain position.[14]

This is really just a couple dance in a group formation. There are no join together or exchange partner figures. It is a couple performance merely reminiscent of an older form with which the dancers may still identify, though they can no longer perform it.

A similar response may be seen in the phenomenon of "Newfy" clubs and music in Toronto, which support such performers as Michael T. Wall, "The Singing Newfoundlander," Harry Hibbs, and many others. The influence of mass media stereotyping, university courses in Newfoundland culture, visiting collectors, and returned emigrants, has contributed to a local awareness and conception of "Newfoundland culture" which is becoming increasingly identified as a separate category of behavior with its own appropriate occasions for expression.

Weddings also continue to be occasions at which the older dance traditions are often performed. As a particularly significant rite of passage, weddings are naturally conservative events. They involve a wide age range of participants and so preserve many older forms. Until recently, as an informant from Wabush, Labrador commented, a wedding was not considered complete unless there were a few square dances and step dances.[15]

During my field work in Plate Cove, Larry Barker's daughter married a man from Plate Cove West, and the wedding reception was held at Brennan's. A band was hired to play modern dance music for most of the evening, but during their breaks, Larry and Gerald played and some square dancing was done, primarily by the older people. Although a few younger people took part, they didn't really know the dance.[16]

At a wedding reception in St. John's on June 21, 1980, I observed several fragments of the Square Dance and a more extended Kissing Dance performance. The wedding party was attended by a number of the groom's friends and relatives from Red Cliff, among them Gerald Quinton and Larry Barker who had been asked to play music. Only four couples out of the hundred or so people there attempted the Square Dance and that without much success beyond the first two bars.

The Kissing Dance was instigated by the groom, the idea, apparently, being to get everyone involved. The partner choosing portion continued for some time, eliciting a variety of responses from those approached, including one high point at which a priest was kissed, amidst great hilarity, and joined the line of dancers. Eventually, a majority of participants had been included, those left out making it clear they did not wish to join in, but by that time dancers were losing interest and leaving the set. The final group figures were not attempted.

The most successful traditional performance of the evening was a step dance by Lloyd Oldford, but he did not command the attention of very many in the room. Several waltz melodies elicited the most response from the dancers, who filled the floor in couples and sang the choruses as they danced. The dancing at this event seemed to reflect a desire to affirm some connection with the groom's family roots in Red

Cliff, but an unfamiliarity with the dance forms among the majority of the participants, who were not from Red Cliff, prevented the successful incorporation of these dance traditions.[17]

New Dances at Old Events

The community festivals, when they are observed at all, no longer provide occasion for dancing the group dances. The garden party, for example, once such an important event, has declined until only one was held in the Plate Cove region, in King's Cove, in 1979. Although a relative of Larry Barker's arranged for him and Gerald to play instead of hiring a band, it seems the square dancing was not very successful.[18]

Mrs. Keough noted that when bands became popular for dancing, "they changed everything," and explained that

> right now they don't have any garden parties because the majority of the younger people, they like the bands. And, it's no good to the older people and plus it's quite a lot of money . . . not worth your money. 'cause that's two hundred and fifty. three hundred dollars.[19]

Other festivals have changed similarly. While in the old days there were probably several large dance event gatherings during the Christmas and winter season, according to Mrs. Keough, "they have the clubs and it's different now." She described the New Year's Balls as held in the clubs nowadays as follows:

> Well, you know, they have a band there . . . . Sometimes you have to get your ticket. you know, about two months beforehand. And, you don't have no, nothing to eat. except. they have cold plates there, you know, if you want them. Go up to the bar and get the cold plate see. And, twelve o'clock, you know, it's all decorated with balloons and everything, so twelve o'clock, whoever you're facing then you give them the great big, you have the little hats on, eh, you has a great big kiss. Give them the great big kiss. Then you burst them [the balloons] . . . . There's sometimes they do have the accordion, somebody who's there with the accordion. Probably Jim Philpott there with the accordion. Next thing you're out and, while the band

is taking a break, you get out and have a go at it. It's really, you know, fun. You meet each other.[20]

These began in Plate Cove after the clubs opened, about five
or six years ago, she recalls. Similar New Year's Balls were
held in Gander, where she worked during 1947 through '51,
with "Canadians and Americans" in civil aviation.[21] This is
another example of the influence of mainland culture during and following the Second World War.

Comments contrasting the dances formerly typical at
larger dance events and the modern dances are common and
usually emphasize the same differences. For example, an informant said the following of Harbour Deep dances in recent years:

> The Goat has just about disappeared and is replaced with
> a few belly rubs, a swing or two, a bit of arm swinging
> and finger cracking and the dance is over.[22]

This comment disparagingly catalogues the important
choreographic changes from the older group form. The new
dances are shorter in duration, they are primarily mixed-sex
couple interactions, movements are more sexually explicit,
with more freedom generally in the use of the body and limbs.
The modern dances are not suited to expression of the social
relations and integrative goals to which the festival events
addressed themselves.

Old Dances at New Events

The group dances are found today in radically different
social settings than those in which they acquired their
characteristic forms. Contemporary performances of the
group dances are most common at self-consciously "cultural"
events. Such events range in formality from the house parties for visiting relatives, noted earlier, to such events as dance
workshops, folk festivals, and media events. This cultural
"revival," to use the term commonly applied to these expressions, may be expressed in other, naturally occurring
events, as, for example, at the wedding described above.
Most commonly, however, dance performances of this type
occur at special events consecrated to promoting and
publicizing the ideals of the cultural "revival."

113

The organization of the dance performances within these new events is very different from that within the dance events of the past. These dances are most often stage performances for an audience. While performing the dancers must interact with one another, but the primary focus of their performance is external and directed toward a nondancing audience. The dances are performed by a small group of interested and skilled dancers. At the older dance events, in contrast, all participants were potential dancers and their performances were internally focused.

Some of the dynamics at work in the process by which the cultural revival movement recruits performers and the impact it may have at a local level may be seen in the experience of the Red Cliff Dancers, as told to me by Mrs. Keough.[23]

Her involvement with the group began with the event which first brought them together as performers. This was the taping of a CBC *Land and Sea* program conceived by the producer Dave Quinton, Gerald's nephew. The program was made in December of 1976 and entitled "A 'Time' in Red Cliff." As Therese told it:

> My brother and a couple from here [Plate Cove] was supposed to go down. They were asked to go down and then some of the boys backed out. I was on the way going to a bingo game when the phone rang. This was Gerald Quinton's wife. They wanted another few from up around here and when the others backed out, from up here, she said, "Well I'll find somebody." So she phoned me. She said, "How would you like to come down," she said, "and go on *Land and Sea*." I said, "Okay, have somebody come up for myself and my brother," I said, "and we won't be long," I said "going down." [Someone] came up here in the van, the CBC van and we went down. And the CBC crowd were out and we had a grand time that time. We had a wonderful time.

Significantly, the program was conceived outside the community and brought to fruition through the efforts of Gerald and his wife, Hilda. They were able to draw upon knowledge of the local people to assemble a willing crowd of participants. That Gerald's family should play this role is no surprise. Merchant families have always been in an intermediary position

114

in the outport communities.

Therese's description of the program itself is also interesting, as it identifies and focuses on several signifiers of the "old times":

> It was in the old hall in Red Cliff. The old FPU Hall, the union hall. We had an old-fashioned stove and an old tea kettle all blackened up, and used to have that round chunks of wood like the old-fashioned. And had the kettle on and the water boiling. And we had a drop of whiskey and rum. We used to make a drop of punch. We used to get the hot water and sugar and make, you know, the old-fashioned. So then they started singing songs. Then we start dancing. Then we had to do the Kissing Dance.

The event self-consciously sought to evoke images of the "old-fashioned" times, and all were aware of this purpose. The last big dance of a similar sort had actually been held six or seven years before.

After this initial contact with the cultural revival outside the community context, a number of collectors, enthusiasts, students and popularizers began appearing on her doorstep. The folk revival group Figgy Duff, while on tour and performing in King's Cove, heard about the Keoughs from their appearance on *Land and Sea* and came to visit. As Therese relates:

> They all came here anyway, they all came here one day. And I just got enough of dinner on for our own selves. I know what I had. I had salt beef and turnip and dumplings, baking-powder dumplings, and jam. And when they come what we did was shared it up with them. And they really enjoyed it, they did.

Shortly after, Aidan O'Hara, an Irishman working for CBC, undergraduate folklore student at Memorial University, and enthusiastic promoter of "folk arts" turned up:

> Aidan O'Hara come knocked to the door and he asked for Cyril Keough. When I seen him, it was the first time I met him, "I said, "Are you Aidan O'Hara?" And he said, "Yes." Well I knew the Irish accent I guess, but I saw him on television. So he came in here. He came in. So then he opened the school and we had a big dance and everything you know.

This would have been one in a series of "grand times" the St. John's Folk Arts Council was then sponsoring in outport communities.

Her story continues:

> In February of that year when we had to go in for a workshop at the LSPU Hall [in St. John's]. That's when we started the real thing. And we were in for two days. Two days, two nights that time.

In subsequent years, she received phone calls to ask the Red Cliff crowd, as they became known, to appear at folk festivals each summer. I first met them at one of these which was held in Bannerman Park, St. John's, during 1979. Therese recalled that subsequently:

> There was three or four, I don't know who they were, strangers I know, but they asked us did I want to come in and give five lessons on the Square Dance. But you know you want time for that.

In 1980, although Therese was anxious to participate, the others decided not to attend the festival. Lloyd Oldford was busy fishing, and Larry Barker and Gerald Quinton had just spent a week in St. John's after attending the wedding described previously. Such concerns have prevented them from participating in several other folk festivals to which they were invited.

From this narrative it is apparent that the Red Cliff Dancers were formed in response to stimuli largely external to the communities they represent. In fact, they don't exist as a group within the local context at all. The individuals who became involved in performing do not interact much on an everyday level at home. This was probably the major reason I was never able to get them together as a group to dance during my field work in the Plate Cove region.

The Red Cliff Dancers are typical of one type of performing troupe. These adult groups often perform, with little or no rehearsal, dances which have not been an active social tradition for many years. They often make mistakes in the performance of figures, but usually convey tremendous energy and command of the style as individual dancers.

The second major class of performing troupe, the youth groups, are taught and rehearsed by adult leaders. They usually perform the figures accurately, but often seem awkward and unskilled in their individual dance movements. One student collector commented on the performance of a group of children who were taught the Lancers in Conception Harbour as follows:

> Some of the natural movements and gestures employed by their ancestors are missing . . . . The children seem to lack the refinement, poise and litheness inherent in the steps of older dancers. They execute the steps [i.e. the figures] very well but do not seem to be "feeling" the music.[24]

The traditional dance movement aesthetic seems to be difficult to teach. Training of dancers was formerly informal, based on observation, emulation, and practice from a young age.[25] As a result, the modern children's dance style is not a natural extension of their movement repertoire and they may often appear awkward.

Intentional changes are occasionally made to the dances by these groups, motivated by an understanding of the changed context of their performance. What is satisfying to a group of dancers performing the figures may not be satisfying to an audience watching them perform. Wanda Crocker, for example, leader of the East End Boys and Girls Club Dancers, has shortened repetitions in the Lancers, having each facing couple figure performed only once by either the head or side couples.[26]

Such changes may be explained in terms of the ritualistic stress reduction typical of traditional, internally focused dances versus the theatrical excitation required of those dances with an external focus:

> When a traditional dance is borrowed, especially when it is a non-audience dance, it must be abridged and made theatrically effective to appeal to an audience that does not have appropriate frames of reference for the original context, and which will not respond properly to endless repetition.[27]

Step dancing has also been frequently adapted for stage use. Externally focused as a choreographic form to begin with, the Step Dance already employs many theatrical effects. A typical change made to increase its effectiveness on stage is the use of taps. One dancer, for example, began using taps on his shoes to perform on stage for the St. John's Folk Arts Council. As he said, "There's no point in having someone dancing [when] . . . you see the legs moving but don't get the beat."[28] Groups of step dancers often perform in unison, sometimes moving in choreographed floor patterns, to increase visual impact. Both are adaptations to suit the context of large audience presentations.

In the "local context," step dancing, as noted earlier, has been syncretized with new music and dance forms much more successfully than the group dances. The complexity of its stepping has declined due to the decreased general interest, individual motivation and opportunities for dancers to perform, but it has adopted the mixed-sex couple organization of dance now preferred. Always practised, but not recognized as a specific dance form, couple step dancing is now seen at almost all dance events with any traditional music. The traditional movement style has simply been adapted to the new structural norms.

I would characterize some other performing troupes as revival groups. These are usually composed of young adults who have self-consciously learned the traditional dances. One such group in St. John's is reluctant to change the dances for stage use. In their view, to change the figures would defeat their purpose in performing, since the audience would no longer be seeing an "authentic" Newfoundland dance. The identity of the dance for them lodges almost entirely in its prescribed sequence of figures. They hope that the individual immersion they achieve in the lengthy and repetitious dance will communicate effectively to the audience.[29] In this instance the ideology of the cultural revival is a stronger shaping force than the performance context.

Conclusion

While formerly a part of dance events integral to community life, which have been described as "extended" events, the group dances are now most often performed as part of "contained" events, which are ends in themselves, needing a limited number of practitioners, and using a specific piece of time.[30] Changing culture and functions have altered the older extended events to the point where the dances once integral to them have disappeared from that context. Simultaneously, new, contained events have been created in which the older dances survive, albeit slightly changed to suit their new environment.

These stage performances are in what has been termed a "second existence" as folk dances. They are no longer the common property of a whole community but only of an interested few. Less of an "integral part of community life," learned simply by virtue of participation in community life, the dances must now be taught more formally and are relatively fixed in performance.[31]

The former freedom of form in Newfoundland dancing is best exemplified by the many traditional variants of the same structural form which have been recorded. Individual dancers were familiar with a repertoire of figures or floor pattern movement units, and the frameworks within which they could be performed. Musical accompaniement was varied as well within the confines of the traditional aesthetic norms. When learned primarily for stage presentation, this flexibility is lost and the dancers and musicians work to polish a set routine to perfection.

Anya Royce has noted that some dances are used formally as symbols of identity especially on occasions when more than one cultural group interacts.[32] These contrast with informal dances which are used for recreation. Although step dancing has been adapted to the stage frequently, it is the group dances which seem to fulfill this role most often. Floor patterns are more easily learned than the movement control necessary for good step dancing, making these dances more accessible to the youth and revival groups most likely to perform them. Yet these dances still "require more technical skill than the average individual in the particular culture possesses," which is another characteristic of such formal dances. Although they were once informal recreational dances, knowledge of the group dances is now very limited. Royce observes further that in order to gain status most groups generally choose "symbols that will be accorded prestige by both outsiders and members of one's own group." This choice is conditioned, however, by the identity one wishes to symbolize.

I attended a May 1981 meeting for leaders of 4H Club youth groups from throughout Canada held in St. John's at which this was strikingly demonstrated.[33] One group, the 4H Club Dancers from Fox Harbour, Placentia Bay, performed versions of the Square Dance, Lancers, and choreographed group step dancing. They were introduced as demonstrating their heritage of Newfoundland dancing. From the community of Dunville, only a few miles away from Fox Harbour, a group of young teenaged girls called the Eager Beavers, performed a disco dance routine to a Bee Gees' recording. Two more different identities could not have been juxtaposed, yet both used dance in the same way to express the performers' conception of themselves to the visiting 4H Club representatives.

The meaning of the group dances in these new contexts, their significance to the audience and performers, even the objective experience of dancing them is very different from that discussed in connection with their first existence. Nevertheless, they still symbolize by similar means. The various movements through which the dancers once enacted their social relations and cultural values serve now in the new contexts as a metaphor for that very experience. The dance forms in their new contained event context stand for the ethos of the older extended events of which they were part. These folk dances have come to represent a cultural ideal with which many Newfoundlanders wish to identify.

NOTES — CHAPTER 4

1. Royce, pp. 110-31.

2. Louie W. Attebery, "The Fiddle Tune: An American Artifact," in *Readings in American Folklore*, ed. Jan Harold Brunvand (New York: W.W. Norton, 1979), pp. 332-33; Feintuch, pp. 64-65.

3. Royce, pp. 76-85.

4. This change is related to that noted by Feintuch in Kentucky, from four couple squares to large circle forms. See Feintuch, pp. 64-65.

5. MUNFLA, Ms., 81-271/p. 329.

6. For a parallel see Bruce Taylor, "Shake, Slow and Selection: An Aspect of the Tradition Process Reflected by Discotheque Dances in Bergen, Norway," *Ethnomusicology*, 24 (1980), 75-84.

7. MUNFLA, Ms., 81-271/p. 168.

8. MUNFLA, Ms., 79-630/pp. 31-32.

9. The following description is condensed and quoted from MUNFLA, Ms., 79-714. This collection was made using a Newfoundland dance questionnaire guide which I prepared.

10. Telephone interview with Gerald Quinton, 27 December 1980.

11. MUNFLA, Ms., 81-271/pp. 196-97; Tape, 81-271/C5194.

12. MUNFLA, Ms., 81-271/p. 258.

13. MUNFLA, Ms., 80-118/p. 31.

14. (Bert Everett), *Complete Calls and Instructions for Fifty Canadian Square Dances as Called by Bert Everett, Port Credit Ontario* (Toronto: Dancecraft, 1977), p. 130.

15. MUNFLA, Ms., 71-74/p. 3.

16. MUNFLA, Ms., 81-271/pp. 175, 178.

17. MUNFLA, Ms., Tape, 81-271/C5180.

18. MUNFLA, Ms., 81-271/p. 92.

19. MUNFLA, Ms., 81-271/pp. 87-88.

20. MUNFLA, Ms., 81-271/p. 113.

21. MUNFLA, Ms., 81-271/p. 17.

22. MUNFLA, Ms., 75-10/pp. 60-61.

23. The following narrative may be found in full in MUNFLA, Ms., 81-271/p. 111.

24. MUNFLA, Ms., 80-118/p. 40.

25. Kealiinohomoku, ''Theory and Methods,'' pp. 255-57, distinguishes informal, formal, and technical training.

26. MUNFLA, Ms., 81-271/pp. 415-16.

27. Kealiinohomoku, ''Theory and Methods,'' pp. 108-109.

28. MUNFLA, Ms., 79-339/p. 29-30.

29. Personal communication from Cathy Ferri, August, 1981. This group has had many names, most recently the Sheila's Brush Dancers.

30. Kealiinohomoku, ''Theory and Methods,'' pp. 236-37.

31. Felix Hoerburger, ''Once Again on the Concept of 'Folk Dance','' *Journal of the International Folk Music Council*, 20 (1968), 30-32.

32. Royce's discussion is in her *Anthropology of Dance*, p. 164.

33. MUNFLA, Ms., 81-271/pp. 405-14.

WORKS CITED

Abrahams, Roger D. "Towards an Enactment-Centered Theory of Folklore." In *Frontiers of Folklore*. Ed. William Bascom. Boulder, Colo.: Westview Press, 1978, pp. 79-120.

Ashton, John. "Some Thoughts on the Role of Musician in Outport Newfoundland." Folklore Studies Association of Canada Meeting. Halifax, 22 May 1981.

Attebery, Louie W. "The Fiddle Tune: An American Artifact." In *Readings in American Folklore*. Ed. Jan Harold Brunvand. New York: W.W. Norton, 1979, pp. 324-33.

Botkin, B.A. *The American Play-Party Song*. 1937; rpt. New York: Frederick Ungar, 1963.

Brady, Chris. "Appalachian Clogging." *English Dance and Song*, 43, No. 1 (1981), 12-13.

Breathnach, Breandán. *Folkmusic and Dances of Ireland*. Dublin: Talbot Press, 1971.

Brunvand, Jan. *The Study of American Folklore: An Introduction*. 2nd ed. New York: W.W. Norton, 1978.

Casey, George. "Traditions and Neighborhoods: The Folklife of a Newfoundland Fishing Outport." M.A. Thesis, Memorial University of Newfoundland, 1971.

Chappell, William. *The Ballad Literature and Popular Music of the Olden Time*. 2 vols. 1859; rpt. New York: Dover, 1965.

Chiaramonte, Louis. "Mumming in 'Deep Harbour'." In *Christmas Mumming in Newfoundland*. Ed. H. Halpert and G.M. Story. Toronto: University of Toronto Press, 1969, pp. 76-103.

Dommett, Roy. "The Kitchen Lancers." *English Dance and Song*, 41, No. 3 (1979), 7.

Doucette, Laurel. "Folk Festival: The Gatineau Valley Church Picnic." *Culture & Tradition*, 1 (1976), 55-62.

Evening Telegram. St. John's, Nfld. 11 Dec. 1879 [p. 1], col. 2; 16 Feb 1900 [p. 3], col. 2.

[Everett, Bert]. *Complete Calls and Instructions for Fifty Canadian Square Dances as called by Bert Everett, Port Credit, Ontario*. Toronto: Dancecraft, 1977.

Faris, James C. *Cat Harbour: A Newfoundland Fishing Settlement*. Newfoundland Social and Economic Studies, No. 3. St. John's: Institute for Social and Economic Research, Memorial University of Newfoundland, 1972.

Feintuch, Burt. "Dancing to the Music: Domestic Square Dances and Community in South Central Kentucky (1880-1940)." *Journal of the Folklore Institute*, 18 (1981), 49-69.

Goffman, Erving. *Behavior in Public Places: Notes on the Social Organization of Gatherings*. New York: The Free Press, 1963.

Gomme, Alice Bertha. *The Traditional Games of England, Scotland and Ireland*. 2 vols. 1894, 1898; rpt. New York: Dover, 1964.

"Good Entertainment '77, Part B." Memorial University of Newfoundland Educational T.V., cat # 10 304, 1979.

Halpert, Herbert and G.M. Story, eds. *Christmas Mumming in Newfoundland*. Toronto: University of Toronto Press, 1969.

Hanna, Judith Lynne. "Toward Semantic Analysis of Movement Behavior: Concepts and Problems." *Semiotica*, 25 (1978), 77-110.

_____. *To Dance is Human: A Theory of Non-verbal Communication*. Austin: University of Texas Press, 1980.

Hoerburger, Felix. "Once Again on the Concept of 'Folk Dance'." *Journal of the International Folk Music Council*, 20 (1968), 30-32.

Howe, Elias. *Howe's Complete Ball-Room Hand Book: Containing Upwards of Three Hundred Dances, including all the Latest and Most Fashionable Dances*. Boston: Elias Howe, 1858.

"Introduction to Fogo Island." National Film Board of Canada, No. 106B 0168 065, n.d.

Ives, Edward D. *Lawrence Doyle: The Farmer Poet of Prince Edward Island. A Study in Local Songmaking*. University of Maine Studies, No. 92. Orono, Maine: University of Maine Press, 1971.

Janković, Ljubica. "Paradoxes in the Living Creative Process of Dance Tradition." *Ethnomusicology*, 13 (1969), 124-28.

Johnston, Thomas F. "Alaskan Eskimo Dance in Cultural Context." *Dance Research Journal*, 7 (1975), 1-11.

Karpeles, Maud. *Twelve Traditional Dances*. London: Novello, 1931.

_____. *Folksongs from Newfoundland*. London: Faber & Faber, 1971.

Katz, Ruth. "The Egalitarian Waltz." *Comparative Studies in Society and History*, 15 (1973), 368-97.

Kealiinohomoku, Joann. "Folk Dance." In *Folklore and Folklife: An Introduction*. Ed. Richard Dorson. Chicago: University of Chicago Press, 1972, pp. 381-404.

_____. "Dance Culture as a Microcosm of Holistic Culture." In *New Dimensions in Dance Research: Anthropology and Dance (The American Indian)*. Ed. Tamara Comstock. New York: Committee on Research in Dance, 1974, pp. 99-106.

_____. "Theory and Methods for an Anthropological Study of Dance." Diss. Indiana University, 1976.

Mannion, John. "Introduction." In *The Peopling of Newfoundland.* New-foundland Social and Economic Papers, No. 8. Ed. John Mannion. St. John's: Institute of Social and Economic Research, Memorial University of Newfoundland, 1977, pp. 1-13.

Margaret, Len [Mary Pittman]. *Fish & Brewis, Toutens and Tales: Recipes and Recollections from St. Leonard's, Newfoundland.* Canada's Atlantic Folklore and Folklife Series, No. 7. St. John's: Breakwater, 1980.

Maritime History Group. *Check List of Research Studies Pertaining to the History of Newfoundland in the Archives of the Maritime History Group, Fourth Edition with Accessions Since October 1975.* n.p.: n.p., March 1981. In the Centre for Newfoundland Studies at Memorial University of Newfoundland.

Nemec, Thomas. *Index to the Archive of Undergraduate Research on New-foundland Society and Culture.* St. John's: Institute for Social and Economic Research, Memorial University of Newfoundland, 1978.

Nevell, Richard. *A Time to Dance.* New York: St. Martin's Press, 1977.

O'Keefe, J.G. and Art O'Brien. *A Handbook of Irish Dances: With an Essay on Their Origin and History.* Dublin: M.H. Gill, 1954.

O'Neill, Capt. Francis. *Irish Folk Music: A Fascinating Hobby.* 1910; rpt. Darby, Pa.: Norwood Editions, 1973.

Pocius, Gerald. "Calvert: A Study of Artifacts and Spatial Usage in a New-foundland Community." Diss. University of Pennsylvania, 1979.

Population Returns 1836. St. John's, 1836. Photocopy in the Centre for New-foundland Studies at Memorial University of Newfoundland.

Public Ledger and General Newfoundland Advertiser. St. John's, 29 May 1857 [p.2], col. 4.

Quigley, Colin. "Folk Dance and Dance Events in Rural Newfoundland." M.A. Thesis, Memorial University of Newfoundland, 1981.

_____. "Singles, Doubles, and Triples: Musical Terminology in Placentia Bay." Folklore Studies Association of Canada Meeting, Montreal, June 1980.

Richardson, Philip J.S. *The Social Dances of the Nineteenth Century in England.* London: Herbert Jenkins, 1960.

Robertson, Margaret. "The Newfoundland Mummers' Christmas House-Visit." M.A. Thesis, Memorial University of Newfoundland, 1979.

Royce, Anya Peterson. *The Anthropology of Dance.* Bloomington: Indiana University Press, 1977.

Ryan, Jacquey. "Dancing in Tack's Beach with Mrs. E. Best." Unpublished Ms., 1980.

Schell, John M. *Prompting: How to Do It.* 1890; rpt. New York: Carl Fischer, 1948.

Sharp, Cecil J. and A.P. Oppé. *The Dance*. London: Halton and Truscott Smith; New York: Minton, Balch and Co., 1924.

"A Square Dance." Memorial University Extension Media Services, 1979.

Story, G.M., W.J. Kirwin, J.D.A. Widdowson, eds. *Dictionary of Newfoundland English*. Toronto: University of Toronto Press, 1982.

Strutt, Joseph. *The Sports and Pastimes of the People of England*. 1801, 1903; rpt. Bath: Firecrest, 1969.

Taylor, Bruce H. "Shake, Slow and Selection: An Aspect of the Tradition Process Reflected by Discotheque Dances in Bergen, Norway." *Ethnomusicology*, 24 (1980), 75-84.

"A Time in Red Cliff." *Land and Sea*. Canadian Broadcasting Corporation, n.d.

Tizzard, Aubrey M. *On Sloping Ground: Reminiscences of Outport Life in Notre Dame Bay, Newfoundland*. Memorial University Folklore and Language Publications, Community Studies Series, No. 2. Ed. J.D.A. Widdowson. St. John's: Memorial University of Newfoundland, 1979.

Wareham, Wilfred W. "Social Change and Musical Tradition: The Role of Singing in the Life of a Newfoundland Traditional Singer." M.A. Thesis, Memorial University of Newfoundland, 1972.

Wolford, Leah Jackson. *The Play-Party in Indiana*. Indiana Historical Society Publications, Vol. 20, No. 2. Ed. & rev. W. Edson Richmond and William Tillson. Indianapolis: Indianapolis Historical Society, 1959.

ARCHIVAL SOURCES CITED

The Archive of Undergraduate Research on Newfoundland Society and Culture (AURN) at Memorial University of Newfoundland.

Philpott, Kevin. "The Importance of the Community Wharf in the Social and Economic Life of Plate Cove East." Ms., No. 333. In AURN.

Tracey, Cecilia. "Sprees in Tickle Cove, Bonavista Bay." Ms., No. 438. In AURN.

Maritime History Group Archives (MHGA) at Memorial University of Newfoundland.

Muggeridge, Wayne. "A Study of the Community of Red Cliff, Bonavista Bay." Ms. in MHGA.

The Memorial University of Newfoundland Folklore and Language Archive (MUNFLA).

MUNFLA, Tape, 65, 65-17/C161-62.

Tape, 66-25/C318.

Ms., 68-4.

Ms., 68-5.

Tape, 72-113/C1131.

Ms., 72-124.

Ms., 72-155.

Ms., 73-75.

Ms., 73-89.

Ms., 73-147.

Ms., 73-158.

Ms., 73-174.

Ms., 74-46.

Ms., 75-25.

Ms., 77-112.

Ms., 77-149.

Ms., 77-155.

Ms., 77-283.

Ms., 77-334.

Ms., 78-003.

Ms., 78-71.

Ms., 78-186.

Videotape, 78-364/v. 39, 42.

Tape, 79-54/C3957, 4107, 4108.

Tape, 79-194/C5112.

Ms., 79-339; Videotape, 79-339/v. 56.

Ms., 79-630.

Ms., 80-41.

Ms., 80-118, includes film.

Videotape, 80-126/(not yet assigned).

Ms., 81-271; Tape, 81-271/C5180-95, 5257-61.

Ms., 81-336.

Q71B-4, 5 and 6; includes Ms., 71-87.

The Newfoundland Dictionary Centre at Memorial University of New-foundland also made its files available to me.